JOHN C. PORTAVELLA

THE LITTLE MANUAL

FOR

SPIRITUAL
GROWTH

SOPHIA INSTITUTE PRESS
MANCHESTER, NEW HAMPSHIRE

Copyright © 2019 by John C. Portavella

Printed in the United States of America. All rights reserved.

Cover by David Ferris Design.

On the cover: green tree (86809207) © Olivier Le Moal / Shutterstock.

Scripture quotations are taken from the Revised Standard Version of the Bible: Catholic Edition, copyright © 1965, 1966 the Division of Christian Education of the National Council of the Churches of Christ in the United States of America. Used by permission. All rights reserved.

Quotations from English translations of papal encyclicals are from the Vatican website (http://w2.vatican.va/content/vatican/en.html) © Libreria Editrice Vaticana. All rights reserved. Used with permission.

No part of this book may be reproduced, stored in a retrieval system, or transmitted in any form, or by any means, electronic, mechanical, photocopying, or otherwise, without the prior written permission of the publisher, except by a reviewer, who may quote brief passages in a review.

Nihil obstat: Rev. Fr. Mark Emman H. Sese, *Censor*
Diocese of Pasig, Philippines
Imprimatur: Most Rev. Mylo Hubert C. Vergara, D.D.
Bishop of Pasig, Philippines

Sophia Institute Press
Box 5284, Manchester, NH 03108
1-800-888-9344

www.SophiaInstitute.com

Sophia Institute Press® is a registered trademark of Sophia Institute.

Library of Congress Cataloging-in-Publication Data

Names: Portavella, John C., author.
Title: The little manual for spiritual growth / John C. Portavella.
Other titles: Planning the journey of life
Description: Manchester, New Hampshire : Sophia Institute Press, 2019. |
   Originally published under title: Planning the journey of life. Phoenix,
   AZ : Leonine Publishers, 2017. | Includes bibliographical references.
Identifiers: LCCN 2019012270 | ISBN 9781622828166 (pbk. : alk. paper)
Subjects: LCSH: Spiritual formation — Catholic Church.
Classification: LCC BX2350.3 .P67 2019 | DDC 248.4/82 — dc23 LC record available at
https://lccn.loc.gov/2019012270

First printing

THE LITTLE MANUAL FOR SPIRITUAL GROWTH

This book is dedicated to
Saint Josemaría Escrivá,
Blessed Álvaro del Portillo,
Bishop Javier Echevarría,
and Monsignor Fernando Ocáriz,
as a token of gratitude for their loving paternity
in successive periods of time.

It is also dedicated to my parents,
José María Portavella
and María Casanova,
who, with awesome faith
and stouteartedness,
gladly made it possible.

CONTENTS

ACKNOWLEDGMENTS

I wish to express my heartfelt gratitude to all those who, in different ways, have contributed to the making of this book.

I will not attempt, here, to give due credit nominally to every one of them. I am sure, though, that God has known perfectly their efforts and will not fail to reward them very well.

Nonetheless, I have to make an exception with Jose Maria Mariano, Ph.D., President of the University of Asia and the Pacific, under whose auspices this book comes to light; Veronica Esposo Ramirez, Ph.D., CRC Director for Operations; Mrs. Erlinda Paez and Divine Angeli P. Endriga, who patiently helped in the editing of this work; as well as Dr. Paul Dumol, Mr. Marcelo de la Cruz, and Mr. Rafael Lobrin, who gave of their precious time to the task of reviewing and revising the text; and the late Col. Eduardo Ungson, Mr. Antonio Jon, Mr. Walter Brown, V. Pacquing Junt, and Mr. Wilson Ledesma, who also contributed to make this project a reality.

May the hidden God repay all of them a hundredfold.

INTRODUCTION

I am the Way.

John 14:6

Though hidden, God is a loving Father who follows our every action with utmost interest. A few of our actions are important and consequential according to human standards. Most of them, however, are not. They are ordinary, prosaic; they may be monotonous and even boring. And yet they are potentially very great and truly significant for receiving eternal life. But in order to achieve that, we have to learn to transform these actions into an offering to God, our hidden Father.

When Jesus Christ, the visible image of the invisible God, came to this earth more than twenty centuries ago, He not only redeemed us and regained for us the condition of being loved as adopted children of God; He also taught us the way to transform ordinary things and events in our lives into opportunities to please the Triune God, the hidden Examiner of our endeavors.

When our Lord came to this world, before His public life, He did not work extraordinary feats, except for the episode in the Temple when He was twelve years old (Luke 2:41–50). Most of the time, His life did not differ very much from ours. He acted with naturalness, which corresponds to His condition as "perfect man," and He liked to refer to Himself as "the son of man."

If we want to give ordinary things a supernatural value, we have the perfect model in Jesus Christ. He redeemed us not only in His Passion and Death on Mount Calvary but in all His actions, including the most seemingly unimportant ones.

In a similar manner, we are called to co-redeem with our Lord in all the moments and varying circumstances of our lives. For that, however, we need to unite ourselves to Jesus Christ, and through Him, with Him, and in Him, to do the will of God the Father, with the help of the Holy Spirit. In this way, we can become an everlasting gift to the Almighty.

To make such a lofty ideal a reality, we need to take concrete steps that will lead us to that high goal. This book attempts to achieve this aim by offering a number of suggestions that might be of help. Practically all of them came from St. Josemaría Escrivá de Balaguer, the founder of Opus Dei, with whom this author had the blessed fortune to reside in Rome from September 1955 to June 1958.

The practices in these pages have immensely helped a great number of people from different walks of life in their quest to achieve union with God in the midst of the most ordinary circumstances of life — that is, to make an epic poem out of ordinary life. In line with St. Josemaría's great love for freedom, however, it is important to emphasize that each person must feel completely free to adopt these suggested practices or to follow different ways on his or her personal, spiritual journey.

Furthermore, these steps are not to be practiced all at once, but step by step, in a way recommended by a prudent spiritual director.

If we have searched for the hidden God and found Him, and more so if we have had the great fortune of discovering Him as revealed in the person of Jesus Christ and His teachings, as authoritatively expounded by the only Church He founded, the Roman Catholic Church, we will have a loving relationship with Him and will help others to do the same.

Introduction

Meanwhile, as we take the test of this life, God continues to be concealed in shadows. This book hopes to be an aid in our relationship with the hidden Lover.

St. Josemaría puts it lucidly when he says, "May you seek Christ, may you find Christ, may you love Christ!"

PLANNING THE JOURNEY OF LIFE

One of the most prized gifts that God has given us is the gift of time. It is precious, for we have only one life to live, which is limited, and our eternal lot depends on how we use it. This is why we should plan well how to fulfill our obligations toward God, our families, our work commitments, our civic duties, and our personal interests, including our rest.

St. Josemaría states categorically: "If you don't have a plan of life, you'll never have order."[1] And he adds: "Virtue without order? Strange virtue!"[2]

Professor Martin Rhonheimer writes:

> The plan of life adapts flexibly to each one's life. It does not add a spiritual structure parallel to ordinary life, but forms a unity with daily normalcy, until it is made into an encounter with God. The plan of life is the concrete and effective primary means to achieve a deep unity of life: unity between work and prayer, between ordinary life and dealings with God.... To faithfully fulfill the plan of life fosters in us the awareness of the nearness of God, and puts us under a permanent "tension" or apostolic "vibration." ...

[1] Josemaría Escrivá, *The Way* (Manila: Sinag-tala Publishers, 1985), no. 76.
[2] Ibid., no. 79.

The Norms are fixed points, concrete things that we resolve to fulfill with constancy and with certain discipline. They are like stone markers or kilometer posts that point out the way, and whose usefulness is shown precisely when there seem to be thousands of human reasons to delay or neglect dealing with God: tiredness, lack of time, excessive work, family problems, urgent tasks, etc.[3]

The effort to fulfill these practices of piety is by far compensated by the advantages derived from it. The words of our Lord apply very well to this case: "my yoke is easy, and my burden is light" (Matt. 11:30).

The Norms of Piety[4] are not to be viewed as mere *means*. Their goal, which is much more important, is union with God. St. Josemaría referred to the Norms when he wrote:

> The truth is, you tell me, "that it's not necessary for me to be a hero or to go to ridiculous extremes in order to persevere when I am forced to be isolated."
>
> And you add, "As long as I fulfill the 'norms' you gave me, I won't worry about the snares and pitfalls of my environment; to fear such trifles — that is what I would be afraid of." Wonderful![5]

---

[3] Martin Rhonheimer, *You Are the Light of the World* (Manila: Sinagtala Publishers, 2010), 202.

[4] The Norms of Piety are practices meant to help Catholics to practice their Faith and be attentive to God throughout each day and amid their daily duties. These practices are the Morning Offering, morning prayer, Holy Mass, spiritual reading, the Angelus, a visit to the Blessed Sacrament, the Holy Rosary, and the examination of conscience.

[5] *The Way*, no. 986.

Urban and modern life moves at a fast pace. We will avoid being dragged by it only if we have a commensurate inner spiritual rhythm given by the Norms of Piety. It is not a matter of reciting prayers quickly for the sake of reciting them, but a matter of truly loving God.

We need to deal with Jesus Christ in friendly terms when following the Norms of Piety in our professional work, in our civic and social lives, and in our rest or playing sports. The life of Christ in us, in our souls, is our strength, our consolation, and our happiness.

But our souls, like our bodies, need to be nourished. Thus, to keep ourselves spiritually healthy, we need to accomplish the Norms of Piety faithfully; if we have missed a norm, we should feel bad, as we would for having skipped a meal for some reason.

If we practice the Norms faithfully, they will become a sure path of contemplative life and sanctity. As St. Josemaría would say, the Norms of Piety are like those tall, red poles that, in very cold countries, are placed along paths that, from time to time, are covered with snow. As long as these signs are taken into account, no one is in danger of falling into a ravine or perishing. And he adds:

> And how shall I acquire "our formation" and how shall I keep "our spirit"? By fulfilling the specific "norms" that your Director gave you, and explained to you, and made you love. Be faithful to them and you'll be an apostle.[6]

The management of time is very important. We need a *plan of life*, a well-thought-out timetable in which there is room for all our duties — to God, to our families, to our work, and to our rest.

Friendship with God, says noted Spanish author Antonio María Ramírez, is sanctity.

---

[6] Ibid., no. 377.

The saints are the friends of God. Sanctity is not the task of geniuses. We can all participate in the divine friendship; we can all know and love Jesus. It is a lifetime project that, thanks to the divine Goodness, is within the reach of all who know how to love. It is a great love, indeed, that could appear to us as beyond our capabilities. But He is the Way, the Truth and the Life.... I invite you to follow, in an orderly manner and little by little, an accessible plan of life that could be adapted to any family or professional situation; and by it you would endeavor to become more useful to God and to others. They are not new things; they are practices that have made saints out of many women and men. They are practices of piety that have sowed human history with peace and joy. They require a commitment to demand from oneself a bit more every day. They need constancy and, at the same time, humility and good humor. It is a commitment to love God, who loves us very much and who is always waiting for something more, even if it is only a few words such as "I love you," in the midst of our work.[7]

Andrés Vázquez de Prada wrote:

St. Josemaría taught [that] self-surrender [to God] takes place when the norms are lived; when we cultivate a robust piety, including daily mortification and penance; when we try not to lose the habit of professional work and study; when we are eager to understand the spirit of our apostolate better every day; when discretion (not mysteriousness nor secretiveness) accompanies our work. And, above all, when we are continually conscious of being united in a special

---

[7] Antonio María Ramírez, *Comprometerse* (Madrid: Ediciones Palabra, 2007), 14.

communion of saints, with all those who form part of our supernatural family.[8]

Some are afraid of committing themselves to a plan of life. They mistakenly think that it would rob them of freedom, but it is not the case.

The same author says:

A life of piety will help us to be free from adoring pagan gods: money, luxury, and success, among others. A life of love of God will help us to be free from selfishness and thus to truly love others, without expecting anything in return. God will free us from prejudices and will lead us to seek, to find, and to love the truth and its consequences.[9]

These practices of piety act as "catalytic" agents. This word, coined by Swedish chemist Jöns Jakob Berzelius in 1836, is used to describe chemical reactions that are accelerated by a substance (the catalyst) that is not changed in the process. A small catalyst can produce a large change. In the spiritual life, the Norms of Piety act as catalysts. They could also be compared to an oxygen tank that allows us to move safely in different environments, even when the air is polluted.

The proper fulfillment of the Norms of Piety is something that demands faith. To give priority to these spiritual practices in an ordinary busy day of work requires belief in the veiled God. He is our Father, who watches us all the time and does not deserve to be taken as "second best." The Norms of Piety are to come first in our list of priorities, for they directly pertain to the glory of God. Here applies very well the universally recognized motto: "First things first!" Consequently, the axiom "The norms come first!"

---

[8] Andrés Vázquez de Prada, *The Founder of Opus Dei*, vol. 2 (New York: Scepter Publishers, 2003), 249.

[9] Ibid., 16.

becomes a fitting principle to adopt to guide us in our often-busy lives. For their performance, we are to reserve our best time and place, never what is left over; God deserves it so. They are to be the first in our timetables, as well as in our minds (hierarchy of values) and in our hearts (hierarchy of love). The reason for this is that they provide the connecting supernatural thread that unites all the diverse aspects of our lives. Each one is meant to be a loving encounter with Christ, and they are there to help us become connected and transformed into Him.

These freely adopted practices are never to be taken as if they were "unwanted visitors" that we entertain grudgingly. On the contrary, we are to love doing them, for each one is a personal and intimate encounter with the great Love of our lives.

We are to be faithful to the Norms of Piety. This is particularly true when we find ourselves spiritually weak. These practices of piety should not be abandoned just because we feel dry and without enthusiasm. St. Josemaría explained it lucidly:

> If the thought ever passes through our minds, in the face of effort or dryness that we are "play-acting," our reaction should be to think that the wonderful moment has come to perform a human play for a divine spectator. God is the spectator: the Father, the Son, and the Holy Spirit: the blessed Trinity. And together with God our Lord, the Mother of God and the angels and saints will also be watching us.
>
> We cannot abandon our life of piety, our life of sacrifice and love. When we act out a play for God, for love of Him, trying to please Him; when we "go against the grain"; when we feel we are playing the role of a jester; let us think that we are jesters of God.[10]

---

[10] Josemaría Escrivá, Letter, March 24, 1931, 18–19.

It stands to reason that we should be careful not to "pile the norms up" in the last minutes of the day. If we do so, we run the risk of converting the last portion of the day into something that resembles a "holy hour," which is good in itself, but certainly not the best for a sound and normal family life.

Work and the Norms of Piety are not to be viewed as separate realities. In fact, if we pray much, we will do our work well. St. Josemaría explained it this way:

> We do not lead a double life, but a unity of life, which is simple and strong and in which all our actions are united.
>
> When we respond generously to this spirit, we acquire a second nature. Without realizing it, we are thinking of our Lord all day long, and we feel an impulse to put God into everything, for without Him, nothing would have any attraction. The time then comes when we can't tell where prayer ends and where work begins; for our work is also prayer, contemplation, a true life of mystical union with God without oddities. This is "good divinization."[11]

There should not be piety without work, nor work without piety.

As for the proper priorities, the following anecdote is very telling: In 1997, in Argentina, Bishop Javier Echevarría Rodríguez was asked something like this: "Father, how can I do all the Norms, considering that I am very busy in my profession?" The answer was quick: "Let us invert this. The question should be: 'How can I do my work, after doing all my Norms?'"

Therefore, our guiding principle should never be "What would I like to do now?" or "What do I feel like doing now?" but rather, "What ought I to do now?" or its equivalent, "What is it that God wants me to do at this moment?"

[11] Josemaría Escrivá, Letter, May 6, 1945.

To the question on how to overcome the tension between the Norms of Piety and professional work, the prelate of Opus Dei replied: "We should not separate these realities. We do our work well if we pray much."

These practices of piety adapt themselves to the most varied sets of circumstances. They are not rigid structures, but rather, are flexible programs of life that fit into our daily schedules "as a rubber glove fits the hand of a surgeon," as St. Josemaría was fond of saying. On occasion, we face unforeseen events, and we have to be ready to change our plans. In such cases, it is usually better to fulfill a norm ahead of time than to postpone it.

Moreover, our duties toward our relatives should never be sacrificed on the altar of our professional work. It is a case of what can be called a "professionalitis," a kind of sickness by which a person exaggerates his or her focus on the demands of work, at the expense of other equally or more important concerns. The care for the family God has given us is the most important business that we have on our hands (as St. Josemaría was also fond of saying). Hence, it is wrong to spend so much time in the office working overtime, or being so immersed in professional work that there is hardly any time left for the family. This can lead to disorder, a serious one, that would displease our Lord.

Similarly, our social and civic duties should not be neglected with the excuse that we are "too busy." Helping to foster the common good, each according to his position and role, is an "obligation ... inherent in the dignity of the human person" (CCC 1913). No one may "content himself with a merely individualistic morality."[12] Thus, for instance, it is the mind of the Church that, "as far as possible, citizens should take an active part in public life" (CCC 1915).

---

[12] Second Vatican Council, Pastoral Constitution on the Church in the Modern World *Gaudium et Spes* (December 7, 1965), no. 30.

Planning the Journey of Life

Finally, our personal health, recreation, and rest are not to be neglected either. We are only stewards of our physical endowments, and God expects us to take good care of them for Him. In consequence, we are to see to it that we eat a balanced diet of healthy foods, sleep enough to recover our energy, exercise sufficiently, and have regular medical checkups. In addition, we are to avoid whatever could undermine our health, such as excessive drinking of alcoholic beverages and smoking.

With these ideas in mind, let us consider what an ordinary day could be like.

2

THE FIRST BATTLE (GETTING UP)

A new day begins. The alarm clock sounds. It is time to get up quickly from bed. The moment has arrived to offer the first sacrifice to our Lord. The body says, "No, not yet!" but the soul says, "Yes! It is time!" And the most important part, the soul, must conquer. It is the first of the many affirmations of love that, with God's help, are to come throughout the day. It is not a matter of thinking that we are better than others, but of struggling with ourselves, aware that the sweetest victory is over ourselves, when it is offered to God.

"'The heroic minute.' It is time to get up, on the dot! Without hesitation, a supernatural thought and ... up! The heroic minute; here you have a mortification that strengthens your will and does not weaken your body."[13] St. Josemaría further explains the reason for this practice:

> Conquer yourself each day from the very first moment, getting up on the dot, at a set time, without granting a single minute to laziness. If, with the help of God, you conquer yourself in that moment, you'll have accomplished a great deal for the rest of the day. It's so discouraging to find yourself beaten in the first skirmish![14]

---

[13] *The Way*, no. 206.
[14] Ibid., no. 191.

St. Mark tells us, "And in the morning, a great while before day, he [Jesus] rose and went out to a lonely place, and there he prayed" (1:35). It is in this fashion that our Lord has taught us how to begin the day aright.

It is time to become agile and set sluggishness aside. It is a good moment to say, "I shall serve!" in daring response to Satan's suggestion: "I will not serve!" Together with these first offerings, there could be the first prayer addressed to the entire "company of veiled spectators." First among them is the Triune God, to whom we will offer our entire day, each in our own fashion. Perhaps we could say, like St. Josemaría: "All my thoughts, all my words, all the actions of this day, I offer to You, Lord, and all out of Love."[15] It makes much sense that the day's first thought and first act of love should be for the concealed Lover who is constantly seeking our attention. Giving the Lord our first thoughts and acts of love will be a big boost to our attempts to be with Him throughout the day.

The moment we awake is the time to greet our Lord and thank Him for the gift of a new day. We offer Him all our actions and our entire lives. It is moving to think of the many generations of Christians who have passed along the wonderful custom of offering to God all the actions of the day. The Morning Offering gives meaning and purpose to our whole day. It starts our conversation with the veiled Lord. It is important to offer our work to God; otherwise we are only doing our work for some other goal, such as for the money we get, for the prestige it brings us, and so forth.

The purpose of the Morning Offering is to dedicate every action of the day to God. And every action, except sin, can be offered to Him. St. Paul says, "Whether you eat or drink, or whatever you do, do all to the glory of God" (1 Cor. 10:31). With the Morning

---

[15] *Todos mis pensamientos, todas mis palabras, las obras todas de este día, te ofrezco, Señor, y todo por Amor.*

Offering, all our activities for the day are dedicated to the Lord through a virtual intention acceptable to Him. It is even better if we renew this intention at other moments during the day.

The consciousness that our day has been offered to the veiled Lord is a great help in performing well in our daily struggles. Before the famous Battle of Trafalgar, Admiral Nelson said: "England expects that every man will do his duty." The British soldiers were motivated, for they knew why they were fighting. Likewise, the Morning Offering reminds us of the purpose of our daily actions and of the King we serve.

After this, it is a good moment to address our Lady (and maybe to kiss our brown scapular) and St. Joseph, our guardian angel, the saints, as well as the souls in Purgatory, and to formulate the desire of gaining all the indulgences that our loving Mother, the Church, has granted to us for the day that is beginning.

In a childlike manner (provided we are certain nobody sees us doing it, for they would not understand what we were doing), we might want to wave at them, and perhaps focus our attention on someone from that great multitude of witnesses: a saint of our devotion, a relative, or a friend who has passed away. This contact with the other world is very comforting. If we were to hesitate and think that such a practice would be childish, we need only remember that our Lord said, "Whoever does not receive the kingdom of God like a child shall not enter it" (Luke 18:17).

If medically permitted, that is, if there is no contraindication, taking a cold shower without delay early in the morning could be an excellent sacrifice to offer to the unseen Lord. It is an opportunity to communicate with Him, thus supernaturalizing this daily hygienic practice. It is also an excellent way to drive away possible temptations that may occur at this time.

Surely, to be aware that we are surrounded by a whole "company of witnesses" is an effective way of avoiding sin, as well as feeling well accompanied. The daily rituals we perform routinely, such as dressing and getting ready for the day could be given much worth and meaning if we attach spiritual interactions or aspirations to them — simply put, by praying. For example, we can imitate St. Josemaría, who, while fastening the buttons on his clothing, used to say something like, "Jesus, fasten me to You!"

Physical exercise, such as calisthenics, is another good chance to convert a possibly tedious experience into a spiritually uplifting one.

The trip to a nearby church lends itself to a period of inner and exterior silence with the recollection that the traffic situation allows. Before we begin, while fastening our seat belts, we may invoke our guardian angels, who are among those "unseen witnesses" and who are ever ready to help us. Then, the blessing for a trip recommended by St. Josemaría comes in handy: "Through the intercession of the Blessed Mary, may I have a good trip. May the Lord be in my journey; and may His angel accompany me!"

Waiting at a red light might be a challenge for our patience. Use this time as an opportunity to react supernaturally, perhaps saying to our Lord: "Most Sacred Heart of Jesus, give us peace!" And at a green light: "Holy Mary, our hope, pray for us!"

3

THE FIRST APPOINTMENT (PRAYER)

When we reach the church, it is time for intense communication with the supernatural world. Some minutes of mental prayer will serve well as preparation for the Holy Mass. And if we feel that we do not have the time for it, for we have a lot of pending things, then *we make time* for prayer. First things first! Intense contact with God in our daily periods of prayer will lead us to find Him in the ordinary activities in which we engage.

> We children of God have to be contemplatives: people who, in the midst of the din of the throng, know how to find silence of soul in a lasting conversation with our Lord, people who know how to look at Him as they look at a Father, as they look at a Friend, as they look at someone with whom they are madly in love.[16]

As much as possible, we are to say our prayers at fixed times and with the help of a good book. If we do it in the office, we can tell our coworkers not to disturb us during that time, for we are "in conference"—no visitors, no phone calls. We are communicating with God, who is always ready to talk with us. We do not need to

---

[16] See Josemaría Escrivá, *The Forge* (Manila: Sinag-tala Publishers, 2000), no. 728.

ask for an audience or to make an appointment beforehand. He is always listening, because He loves us infinitely.

It is a matter of conversing with the distinct Persons of the Blessed Trinity, with our Lady, or with anyone in the company of witnesses, which constitutes our splendid family.

What is important is to fall in love with the Lord, to do things that increase our friendship with the Triune God, and to avoid firmly whatever hurts this relationship. For that, the introductory prayer recommended by the founder of Opus Dei is very helpful:

> My Lord and my God, I firmly believe that you are here, that you see me, that you hear me. I adore you with profound reverence; I beg your pardon for my sins and the grace to spend this time of prayer fruitfully. My immaculate Mother, St. Joseph my father and lord, my guardian angel, intercede for me.

Notice that, in this prayer, we remind ourselves of the astonishing fact that God is here! He, the Almighty, sees and hears us perfectly, although we, who are taking the great test of our lives—a test on faith, hope, and love—do not. The situation is very similar to a one-way mirror. He sees us perfectly, but we do not see Him at all.

Observe also that after having expressed our deep respect for Him, we ask pardon for our sins. Our Lord does not listen to us merely because we are very good and behave very well, but because He loves us boundlessly. He is so merciful and His love is so immense that even if we had committed the greatest imaginable crimes, He would still listen to us, provided we were truly repentant of our sins.

St. Josemaría writes, "However unworthy the person, however imperfect the prayer turns out to be, if it is offered with humility and perseverance, God always hears it."[17] He also wrote:

[17] Josemaría Escrivá, *Furrow* (Manila: Sinag-tala Publishers, 2000), no. 468.

If we were to love ourselves excessively, then there would be every reason to be sad, on seeing all our failures and meanness. Such wretchedness might well sadden and discourage us. But if we love God above all things, and if we love others, and ourselves, in God and for God, then we have great reason for rejoicing! ... If ever you feel crestfallen on experiencing your own wretchedness, perhaps in a particularly vivid way, then, it is the moment to be completely docile and abandon yourself totally into God's hands. There is the story of a beggar who came up to Alexander the Great and asked him for alms. Alexander stopped, and commanded the man to be made ruler over five cities. The poor man, overwhelmed and bewildered, exclaimed: "But I did not ask for so much!" And Alexander replied: "You asked according to what you are; I am giving according to what I am."[18]

Thus, in the throes of His Crucifixion, Jesus answered: "Truly, I say to you, today you will be with me in Paradise" to a criminal who had said to Him: "Remember me when you come in your kingly power" (Luke 23:42–43). He did not reply, as we might have expected, with words such as, "I am the Holy One; I do not talk to people like you!"

In the recommended introductory prayer, we also asked that we spend our prayer time fruitfully. This means that we wish to come out of it more united to the Almighty, more resolved to fulfill His will, as perhaps manifested in some specific resolutions. We wish to become more eager to serve others and help them to be happier by discovering our King and His entourage of angels and saints. It means not necessarily that we have had an enjoyable time but, rather, that God was pleased. We might have struggled

[18] Escrivá, *Letter*, March 24, 1931, 24–26.

with distractions and experienced spiritual dryness, but the Lord was pleased in seeing us persevere in our efforts.

As for the content of this friendly conversation with the unseen Lover, the advice of St. Josemaría is, as always, clear and helpful:

> You wrote to me, "To pray is to talk with God. But about what?" About what? About Him, and yourself: joys, sorrows, successes and failures, great ambitions, daily worries — even your weaknesses! And acts of thanksgiving and petitions and love and reparation. In short, to get to know Him and to get to know yourself — get acquainted![19]

As if wanting to emphasize the importance of the awareness of God's presence in genuine prayer, St. Josemaría elaborates: "You don't know how to pray? Put yourself in the presence of God, and as soon as you have said, 'Lord, I don't know how to pray!' you can be sure that you have already begun."[20]

He adds:

> Mental prayer is this heart-to-heart dialogue with God in which the whole soul takes part; intelligence, imagination, memory and will are all involved. It is a meditation that helps to give supernatural value to our poor human life, with all its normal, everyday occurrences.[21]

And as to summarize what this kind of prayer is all about, he writes:

> Do you remember? You and I were praying silently as night was falling. From close by came the murmur of water. And,

---

[19] *The Way*, no. 91.
[20] Ibid., no. 90.
[21] Josemaría Escrivá, *Christ Is Passing By* (Manila: Sinag-tala Publishers, 2000).

through the stillness of the city, we also seemed to hear voices of people from many lands, crying to us in anguish that they do not yet know Christ. Unashamedly you kissed your Crucifix and you asked him to make you an apostle of apostles.[22]

At prayer time, it is useful to bring with us some spiritual book, in case we might need this material as we praise our Lord, express our love and dependence on Him, give thanks for so many blessings we have received, ask pardon for so many offenses and omissions we see upon examining our lives, and ask for things we and our relatives and friends need. If one passage of the book does not impress us particularly, all we have to do is to read on; perhaps another paragraph will help us more.

We need to have faith during this precious time of conversation with the Triune God and His entourage. We have to be convinced that they look at us and love us in spite of our weaknesses and sins, provided that we are truly sorry for our transgressions. The Lord is always there — even when we do not feel His presence.

In other words, we should converse with God not for the sake of experiencing enjoyment and sensible consolations but, rather, to please Him. The Lord is to replace our egos. If we adopt this attitude, we will persevere in prayer even if it turns out to be a dry experience. St. Josemaría puts it this way: "Don't tell Jesus you want consolation in prayer. But if He gives it to you, thank Him. Tell Him always that what you want is perseverance [in prayer]."[23] Yes, oftentimes we will need to remember the complaint of our Lord in Gethsemane: "Simon, are you asleep? Could you not watch one hour?" (Mark 14:37).

---

[22] *The Way*, no. 811.
[23] Ibid., no. 100.

As a good-humored friend of mine once told me, "It is obvious that the purpose of going to pray is not just to feel good, for if this were the case, I would expect spiritual writers to recommend going to prayer with a bottle of liquor, not just with a spiritual book." And as to make his point clearer, he added in the same vein:

There is the story of a businessman who, at noon, went to the Manila cathedral to spend some time in meditation. It was hot, and since it was after lunch, he felt quite sleepy and told our Lord that he was leaving, for he was feeling very far and disconnected from Him. As he was walking toward the door of the church, the organist had started his daily rehearsal, and upon hearing the notes of that beautiful music, he decided to stay, and he told our Lord, "Now I feel very near You!"

Unfortunately, however, after a few minutes there was a brownout, and the electric organ fell silent. And so did the feeling of the businessman, who, turning toward the sanctuary, said, "Lord, I feel far from You again! I am leaving!"

My friend commented that he deserved to have heard a voice coming from the tabernacle telling him, "Come on, do not be so superficial, don't subordinate your prayer life to Meralco!"[24]

The point here is that even though such things as music can help elicit feelings that facilitate prayer, they are not to be taken as an essential and indispensable element for our conversation with our Lord. What is essential is *faith*, which leads to love and hope. With or without feelings, we can always love. For this reason, in prayer, love matters more than thinking. Love benefits from feelings

---

[24] An electric company that supplies electricity to the residents of Manila.

as well as from dryness, from inspirations as well as from aridity. Anything that fosters our love for God is a good subject matter for our prayer.

We see examples of this in the life of our Lord as recorded in the Gospels. We can talk with Him in a very natural way about what is happening in our lives and can silently seek His advice for the decisions we are going to make. What matters most is some awareness — savory fruit of faith — that we are in the presence of the Lord of Lords and His supernatural entourage. Consequently, words are not always needed. We could, at times, simply *give silent company* to the personages of the supernatural world.

When we offer prayers of petition, Leo Trese explains:

> Asking God for our needs, we are not of course telling God something that He does not know. God knows what we need far better than we know ourselves; He has known all our needs from all eternity. A prayer of petition for ourselves focuses our attention on our own necessity and keeps alive our awareness of God's goodness; in prayers of petition for others, we are given the opportunity for limitless acts of charity.[25]

St. Thomas Aquinas further clarifies that prayer of petition makes us stop and realize our smallness and desire the thing we are praying for in a fervent, filial spirit. Thus, we become more worthy to receive it.

Our Lord directed us to pray perseveringly, "We ought always to pray and not to lose heart" (see Luke 18:1). He also pointed out the importance of praying with others: "If two of you agree on earth

[25] Leo Trese, *The Faith Explained* (Manila: Sinag-tala Publishers, 2008), 537.

about anything they ask, it will be done for them by my Father in heaven" (Matt. 18:19).

Our prayers of petition should be persevering and patient. We should not get discouraged because we do not get what we ask for right away. The veiled God wants to give us the chance to earn merits by the testing of our faith, and He allows us to manifest our trust and perseverance. It took St. Monica years of fervent prayer to obtain the conversion of her son Augustine.

Moreover, our prayer should also be full of trust. Pope Benedict XVI has said: "All our prayers — with every possible limitation, effort, poverty, dryness and imperfection they may have — are so to speak purified and reach God's heart. In other words, we can be sure that there is no such thing as superfluous or useless prayers; no prayer is wasted."[26]

Mary is a model of trustful prayer, as evidenced at the wedding in Cana (see John 2:1–11). Moreover, the prayers of the Virgin Mary, in her fiat and her Magnificat, are characterized by the generous offering of her whole being in faith (no. 2622).

On several occasions, the founder of Opus Dei emphasized that there are countless ways of praying. But he would like everyone to pray genuinely, as God's children, not gabbling away like hypocrites who will hear from Jesus' lips: "Not every one who says to me, 'Lord, Lord,' shall enter the kingdom of heaven" (Matt. 7:21). When we cry "Lord!" we must do so with a desire to put into practice the inspirations that the Holy Spirit awakens in our souls.

What is truly important in prayer is to place ourselves in God's presence and to try to remain there. To this effect, it would help to repeat slowly the introductory prayer mentioned above, time and again, until its message registers in our souls. The idea is to

---

[26] Benedict XVI, General Audience, September 12, 2012.

become fully aware that right now, the veiled God is here, in front of me, or at my side, or inside me, for in fact He is everywhere. "One can always enter into inner prayer, independently of the conditions of health, work, or emotional state. The heart is the place of this quest and encounter, in poverty and in faith" (CCC 2710).

Naturally, our spiritual contact with our Lord will enkindle in us a great desire to improve our lives in return for His overwhelming Love. In other words, it will move us to make some specific resolutions to behave much better in the future. In addition, it will move us to perform good deeds, especially those that benefit others, as a practical manifestation of our love for God.

The greatest fruit of this contact with the Lord is that our hearts will grow in love for Him and our commitment to Christ will become deeper. He said: "I came to cast fire upon the earth; and would that it were already kindled!" (Luke 12:49). In prayer, in this conversation with God, we find the strength to overcome tiredness and to reject tepidity.

Moreover, intimacy with God will result in a greater determination to resist temptations and a more persevering apostolic zeal; that is, an eagerness to share happily with others the fruits of our prayer and contemplation. All along, we are convinced that all the sincere prayers are heard, that they are never useless, although they are not always granted in the way we would like.

Consequently, as St. Josemaría suggests, we could end the period of conversation with Jesus by telling Him:

> I give You thanks, my God, for the good resolutions, affections, and inspirations You have communicated to me in this meditation. I beg Your help in performing them. My Immaculate Mother, St. Joseph my father and lord, my guardian angel, intercede for me.

THE LITTLE MANUAL FOR SPIRITUAL GROWTH

This invocation to our Immaculate Mother responds to the great need we have for her help. She is the mother of all Christians—among other reasons—because when she carried our Savior in her womb, she was also carrying all those whose lives were united to Jesus Christ's life.

4

THE PERFECT SACRIFICIAL
MEAL (HOLY MASS)

After this, the Holy Mass begins. We are aware that it is the greatest action we will take part in this day, as well as the best gift that we, in union with Jesus and with the help of the Holy Spirit, can offer to the veiled God the Father. Therefore, in order to be there and to participate in the Holy Sacrifice, we do not hesitate to exert a considerable effort. We realize that it is something truly worthwhile. At the offertory, when the priest lifts the paten, imagine that you place on it all your efforts for the day.

Truly, the Holy Mass is the bloodless re-presentation of the Sacrifice at Calvary. In the Eucharistic Sacrifice and on the Cross, there is the same Eternal Priest and the same Victim of Calvary, Jesus Christ, truly present! Regardless of who is officiating on the altar, the High Priest of every Mass is our Lord Himself. Only He has the divine power to change ordinary bread into His Body, and plain wine into His precious Blood. He transcends time and space.

As an effective and sensible sign, the Holy Mass is also the sacramental memorial of the Last Supper and of the Resurrection of Jesus. In Holy Communion, we receive not only the Body of Christ, but also the Risen Lord. It is, therefore, the sacramental memorial of the Paschal Mystery: the Passion, Death, and Resurrection of Christ. By it, the sacrifice of the Cross is perpetuated over the centuries. It is therefore, at the same time and inseparably, the sacrificial commemoration of the sacrifice of the Cross and the sacred banquet by which we have a most intimate communion with the Lord's Body and Blood.

Fr. Antonio María Ramírez puts it this way:

> We Christians have an unconquerable force: Christ has defeated sin and has changed the meaning of death, and we are reminded of this splendid reality in the Holy Mass. On the altar of the world, in any place, at any time, Jesus climbs up to the Cross. There is nothing better.[27]

The Holy Mass is the perfect sacrifice of adoration, thanksgiving, petition, and reparation offered by Jesus Christ to His eternal Father by the action of the Holy Spirit, and the instrumental cooperation of the priest, in which Jesus acts in His capacity as the Eternal High Priest and Head of His Mystical Body, the Church.

In view of this, it is not surprising that the first of the Church's commandments is: "On Sundays and other holy days of obligation, the faithful are bound to participate in the Mass" (CCC 2180; *Code of Canon Law*, can. 1247). The Church commands this observance as a minimum and under pain of mortal sin, an indication of how important the Holy Mass is for our spiritual lives and our inner growth.

Although mankind all over the world persists in offending God grievously, the continuous offering of Holy Masses offers a mighty ray of hope, for in every Holy Mass Jesus tells His heavenly Father: "Forgive them; for they know not what they do" (Luke 23:34). This realization moved St. Leonard to state:

[27] Ramírez, *Comprometerse*, 58.

I believe that were it not for Holy Mass, at this moment the world would be in the abyss, unable to bear the mighty load of its iniquities. The Holy Mass is the potent prop that holds the world upon its base.

Therefore, when we are participating in it, we ought to do that which once the Portuguese Admiral Alphonse of Albuquerque did, who, finding himself with his fleet in danger of perishing during a fierce and terrific tempest, adopted the following means: He took in his arms an innocent child which was on board his ship, and lifting him up towards heaven, he said, "If we are sinners, this creature is certainly free from sin; Lord, for love of this innocent, remit to us the death we deserve!" Will you believe it? The spectacle of that stainless babe was so pleasing to the Lord that He tranquilized the sea, and changed into joy for these unfortunates their terror of a death already imminent. Now what do you believe is done by the Eternal Father when the priest, lifting in the air the thrice sacred Victim, shows to Him the innocence of His divine Son? Then His compassion cannot resist the sight of the most spotless innocence of Jesus, and He feels as if compelled to calm our storms, and to provide for all our necessities.[28]

In the words of Pope St. John Paul II: "The Eucharistic Sacrifice is the source and summit of all Christian Life. It is a single sacrifice that embraces everything. It is the greatest treasure of the Church. It is Her life."[29]

Accordingly, St. Josemaría Escrivá says, "It brings us face to face with one of the central mysteries of our faith, because it is

---

[28] Leonard of Port Maurice, *The Hidden Treasure of the Holy Mass* (Rockford, IL: TAN Books, 1952), back cover.

[29] John Paul II, Prayer for Priests on Holy Thursday (March 25, 1982).

the gift of the Blessed Trinity to the Church. It is because of this that we can consider the Mass as the center and the source of a Christian's spiritual life."[30]

St. Josemaría advises:

> Think about the Holy Mass—how we should celebrate or attend it. Consider how the Angels are there. Consider that what you are doing or taking part in is something divine. Think how, on the altar, Christ is offering Himself once more for you and for me. And you will earnestly desire to imitate Him in His humility, in the way He empties Himself completely in the Host; and you will be filled with thanksgiving and adoration, desires of reparation, and petitions. You will offer yourself up, your arms outstretched, as another Christ, *ipse Christus* (Christ Himself), ready to be nailed to the sweet wood of the Cross for love of souls.[31]

At the beginning of the Holy Mass, there were on the altar simple bread and plain wine. After the Consecration, the Risen Christ is present, alive, with His sacred Body, His spotless Soul, and His infinite divinity. What a sublime change! Should we not be most eager to be there when it happens? It is worthwhile even if it calls for some sacrifice on our part; that sacrifice will never be comparable to our Lord's sacrifice on Calvary.

This change is effected by the Holy Spirit for our sakes. Our Lord wants to be our nourishment. When we receive Holy Communion, it is not the Eucharist that is transformed into us, but it is we who become spiritually united to Christ. St. Augustine attributes these words to our Lord: "You will not convert Me into

---

[30] *Christ Is Passing By*, no. 87.

[31] Josemaría Escrivá, notes taken from a meditation, April 14, 1960.

yourself, as you transform food into your own flesh: you will be changed into Me."[32]

In light of these considerations, we should try to follow these practices:

- Always get to Holy Mass on time. It is a very good idea to make the Sunday Holy Mass a family event. This should not be the reason, however, for any lack of punctuality. Being punctual is a way of being considerate toward Jesus Christ and toward others who are attending the Eucharistic Sacrifice.

- Dress properly and modestly. Remember that you are meeting with the King of Kings. Women, especially, are to refrain from dressing in such a way that they could lead others to sin. They are to recall that our Lord said: "Every one who looks at a woman lustfully has already committed adultery with her in his heart" (Matt. 5:28).

- Genuflect and bow reverently at the proper places and at the proper time, and stand, sit, and kneel *with* the congregation.

- Maintain reverent silence and a dignified posture in the church. Avoid, for example, receiving Holy Communion with your hands in your pockets— it is too casual and not a respectful attitude. We would not approach and face a high dignitary in this way.

Above all, we are to make sure that our Holy Communion will be a worthy one. Bear in mind these words of St. Paul:

Whoever, therefore, eats the bread or drinks the cup of the Lord in an unworthy manner will be guilty of profaning the

---

[32] St. Augustine, *Confessions* (New York: Image Books, 1960), bk. 7, no. 10.

body and blood of the Lord. Let a man examine himself, and so eat of the bread and drink of the cup. For any one who eats and drinks without discerning the body eats and drinks judgment upon himself. (1 Cor. 11:27–29)

We are to also bear in mind that although it is very good to receive Holy Communion during Mass, it is required only for the priest celebrating. The faithful in the congregation are not required to do so by the laws of the Church. Even without partaking of Holy Communion, participating in the Holy Mass has a great value, significance, and beneficial effects.

Participating actively by uniting ourselves to the Holy Sacrifice at the altar, we are to follow the rites of the Holy Mass and receive Holy Communion while observing the Eucharistic fast, with a conscience that does not accuse us of any mortal sin. Writes Ronald Knox: "The Holy Eucharist is a sun which fosters supernatural life in those who receive it worthily, rain which gives them growth. It is a sun which dries up all life in the souls which receive it unworthily, rain which brings it only corruption."[33]

We are to correspond to the love of Christ, who expressed thus His desire to institute the Eucharist: "I have earnestly desired to eat this passover with you before I suffer" (Luke 22:15). We rightfully express our gratitude to anyone who pays the tiniest service to us. Should we not show much more appreciation to our Lord for the Bread of Life? Here are some ways to do so:

- Put electronic phones and other devices in silent mode. It is irreverent to answer phone calls or send text messages during Holy Mass.
- Maintain respectful silence in the church at all times.

[33] Ronald Knox, *A Retreat for Lay People* (Lagos: Criterion Publications, 2005), 85.

• Stay in the church until the Holy Mass is concluded, and preferably after giving thanks, for about ten minutes. "It should be pointed out to the faithful that, after the Eucharistic banquet, they ought not to neglect to make a sincere and fitting thanksgiving."[34]

If we do these things, the Eucharistic Sacrifice will have an effect in our ordinary lives. For instance, we will work with greater motivation, we will treat others more charitably, and we will have the joy proper of a son or a daughter of God.

---

[34] Sacred Congregation of the Sacraments, *Immensae Caritatis* (January 29, 1973), no. 3.

5

WORK AS USUAL

Now the time has come to go to work. This means facing the traffic situation again. It is rush hour, and everyone seems to be tense. But the period of prayer has helped you a lot for this new challenge. Maybe a taxicab or a motorcycle has come out of nowhere, gotten in your way, and suddenly forced you to apply the brakes. You were tempted to curse the bones of the driver, but you then remembered that, besides bones, he has a soul to save. So, you say a prayer for him: "Lord, help that driver to do a better job; he needs Your help!" And aware that getting mad would not solve any problem, you repress other less supernatural ideas and words that might spontaneously occur to you.

You have arrived at your place of work. There you find the same setting as every day: the same faces, the same furniture, the same environment, day in and day out. It might appear prosaic and unappealing, yet it is precisely *there*, and not somewhere else, that the great Spectator wants you to perform for Him and for the entire supernatural audience. It can become an exciting experience if there is enough faith, hope, and love.

Perhaps you find your colleagues at work chatting before beginning their daily tasks. You, in contrast, are eager to begin to sanctify that work by beginning on time and doing the work well, with all the human perfection you are capable of. For you, punctuality is a good work habit. You have a motivation that others seem to lack:

you are conscious of the fact that you are being constantly looked at by your loving Father. Others are, perhaps, talking negatively about some absent people. You profoundly dislike backbiting, not only because it is unfair, since those persons cannot defend themselves, but because it offends the veiled Father, who loves everyone and wants us to do the same. Upon seizing the situation, convinced that just because something is very common does not mean that it is right, you try to find a way to improve the topic of the conversation.

The workday has begun. It is a good moment to renew the gift of that labor you made in the Morning Offering and in the Holy Mass when you mentally placed on the paten — lifted up by the priest — the work you would carry out during the day. That offering covers all your labor: those things you enjoy doing, as well as the tedious tasks done hour after hour, and also the frustrations and periods of pressure and stress. It also covers the unforeseen happenings that challenge your cool and try your patience. Once more, the teachings of the founder of Opus Dei are of help:

> You are upset. Look: happen what may in your interior life
> or in the world around you, never forget that the importance
> of events or of people is very relative. Take things calmly.
> Let time pass. And then, as you view persons and events
> dispassionately and from afar, you'll acquire the perspective
> that will enable you to see each thing in its proper place
> and in its true proportion. If you do this, you will be more
> objective and you'll be spared many causes of anxiety.[35]

Through work, you joyfully cooperate with God in making this world a better place to live in, and you contribute positively to Jesus' work of Redemption. You do not want to forget that line in the book of Job: "Man is born to labor and the bird to fly" (Job

[35] *The Way*, no. 702.

5:7, Douay-Rheims). For you, work is an obligation rooted in human nature. It was planned by God from the very beginning, even before the fall from Paradise. The Lord placed man in the world so that he would work (see Gen. 3:16). It is clear that work is a good thing for man, because through work man not only transforms nature, adapting it to his needs, but also achieves fulfillment as a human being.

St. Benedict, an ancient saint, has left us an excellent motto as a guide in our journey: Pray and Work! (*Ora et Labora!*) This motto is echoed in the teachings of St. Josemaría, a saint of the twentieth century.

It is obvious that some people work much and very well, but they do not pray. It is a pity, for they seem to have forgotten that no one can please God without praying. Indeed, the Lord urges us to "pray constantly." There are also people who pray much but do not work. God does not approve of this either. They are sometimes called "holy Joes" or "do-gooders," and they do not command respect. Finally, there are others who neither work nor pray. They are, surely, the least pleasing to God.

A true Christian adopts and practices the Benedictine motto, combining the two virtues of prayer and work in unity of life.

Jesus, Mary, and Joseph have left us with a very impressive example of dedication to work. Thus, if out of laziness someone refuses to labor, that person cannot properly call himself Christian. St. Paul's dictum is well known: "If any one will not work, let him not eat" (2 Thess. 3:10). St. Josemaría writes, "You must strive for holiness, contributing at the same time to the sanctification of others, your fellow men; sanctifying your work and your environment."[36] These ideas could be summed up by saying that

---

[36] *Christ Is Passing By*, no. 46.

we are to sanctify our ordinary work, sanctify ourselves in our work, and sanctify others with our work.

The founder of Opus Dei says, "If we really want to sanctify our work, we are inescapably to fulfill the first condition: that of working well, with human and supernatural seriousness."[37]

To sanctify ourselves in our professions or trades, we ought to work seeking the glory of God. This implies a steady exercise of supernatural and human virtues. We can recognize that this seemingly monotonous and perhaps small task has a transcendent co-redemptive value in God's eyes; that is *faith*. Similarly, we *hope* that we will be able to achieve union with God, precisely in and through these daily tasks. And the crowning virtue, *charity*, inclines us to do everything for the love of God.

After that follow a host of moral virtues:

+ *Prudence* helps us to determine the proper means to apply in every instance in order to obtain the right objective.
+ *Justice* leads us to give to each one his due and to fulfill our familial, professional, and social duties.
+ *Temperance* helps us to moderate our tendency to enjoy pleasurable things in excess.
+ *Fortitude* allows us to persevere in fulfilling our professional duties, even when they become strenuous and difficult.
+ *Humility* facilitates seeking, in all our endeavors, not our personal satisfaction, but God's glory.

We could mention many other virtues, such as order, punctuality, and industriousness.

Thus, motivated by love—above all, by divine love—we are moved to work and spend ourselves for others.

Working well is also a means to evangelize, to bring others closer to God. It is a universally recognized fact that people value a job

---

[37] *The Forge*, no. 698.

done well. Our Lord impressed His contemporaries, who exclaimed: "He has done all things well" (Mark 7:37).

Work has great importance. As a task of collaboration and stewardship with the Creator, it is a way to make this world a more humane and livable place, to contribute to a more just social order, and to pursue the temporal common good. In addition, work is also a means and an opportunity to evangelize. It is a *hook* to *fish* souls for Christ. When someone strives to be united to God, to take Christ seriously, he often moves colleagues like him to do the same.

6

A DATE AT NOON (THE ANGELUS OR REGINA COELI)

Noontime is a welcome break. It is a golden opportunity to be faithful to a very brief date with our Blessed Mother.

The Angelus is a wonderful and ancient practice introduced in 1263. It has a long history behind it. Traditionally, the Angelus is prayed at 6:00 a.m., noon, and 6:00 p.m.

The Angelus

The Angel of the Lord declared to Mary:
And she conceived of the Holy Spirit.

Hail Mary, full of grace, the Lord is with thee; blessed art thou among women and blessed is the fruit of thy womb, Jesus. Holy Mary, Mother of God, pray for us sinners, now and at the hour of our death. Amen.

Behold the handmaid of the Lord:
Be it done unto me according to Thy word.

Hail Mary . . .

And the Word was made Flesh:
And dwelt among us.

Hail Mary . . .

Pray for us, O Holy Mother of God, that we may be made worthy of the promises of Christ.

Let us pray. Pour forth, we beseech Thee, O Lord, Thy grace into our hearts; that we, to whom the Incarnation of Christ, Thy Son, was made known by the message of an angel, may by His Passion and Cross be brought to the glory of His Resurrection, through the same Christ Our Lord. Amen.

In our time, the pope appears at noon on Sundays at St. Peter's Square to pray the Angelus with those who have gathered there. In so doing, the Holy Father gives us an example on keeping proper priorities. He interrupts whatever he is doing in order to honor the Virgin Mary. It is an invitation to us to act in a similar fashion while involved in our daily occupations.

The Angelus is a way to cross the *barrier*—exercising our faith—and to converse with our Lady about the role she played in our redemption. We remind her of the great moment of the Annunciation, when the archangel Gabriel made known to her God's plan of salvation and her most exceptional vocation to be the Mother of God. We also remind her and ourselves of her splendid surrender, expressed by her words, "Be it done to me according to your word," which made us brothers of Jesus Christ and heirs of heaven (see Luke 1:26–38). In short, we bring to our minds the sublime mystery of the Incarnation.

From Easter Sunday to Pentecost Sunday, the Regina Coeli (Queen of Heaven) is said instead of the Angelus.

Regina Coeli

Queen of Heaven, rejoice, alleluia.
For He whom you did merit to bear, alleluia.
Has risen, as he said, alleluia.

A Date at Noon (the Angelus or Regina Coeli)

Pray for us to God, alleluia.
Rejoice and be glad, O Virgin Mary, alleluia.
For the Lord has truly risen, alleluia.

Let us pray. O God, who gave joy to the world through the Resurrection of Thy Son, our Lord Jesus Christ, grant, we beseech Thee, that through the intercession of the Virgin Mary, His Mother, we may obtain the joys of everlasting life. Through the same Christ our Lord. Amen.

We can check at this point, after the short noon break, how we are faring in the fulfillment of our resolutions.

7

BRINGING FRIENDS CLOSER TO GOD

Lunchtime is often an excellent opportunity to eat with colleagues and friends and to deepen our bonds with them. Before eating, we say a short prayer to ask God to bless us and the food we are about to eat. Afterward, it is fitting to say a prayer to express to Him our gratitude for all the benefits we have received.

Lunch is a good occasion to interact with friends, to learn their concerns, and to give useful advice in professional as well as spiritual matters. With the help of the guardian angels, you can carry out an effective apostolate of friendship and trust. The founder of Opus Dei says, "Win over the guardian angel of the one you want to draw to your apostolate. He is always a great accomplice."[38]

At the workplace, where much of your time is spent, you meet different kinds of people. Some are a joy to deal with; others, not so much. You manage to meet all of them with a smile. Perhaps, on occasion, someone misunderstands or maltreats you, and you then recall these words of St. Josemaría, "All right: that person has behaved badly toward you. But, haven't you behaved worse toward God?"[39]

In this manner, you manage to carry out the tasks of everyday life with order and serenity and without nervousness. You avoid

[38] *The Way*, no. 563.
[39] Ibid., no. 686.

haste in your gestures, even in the way you climb the stairs. You move the way you would expect from a person with a contemplative spirit. Consequently, those working with you enjoy your company, and perceive you as someone who exudes peace and happiness. If they were to seek the source of it, they would find it in your union and frequent dealings with the veiled Lord, who dwells in secret but continues telling everyone: "Peace be with you!"

After a long day of toil, working intensely and orderly, it is not surprising to feel fatigued. You may be tempted to call it a day and abandon the task a bit before its time. A crucifix or some other discreet human device at your place of work comes in very handy:

> You ask me, "Why that wooden Cross?" And I quote from a letter, "As I raise my eyes from the microscope, my sight comes to rest on the Cross—black and empty. That Cross without a Corpus is a symbol; it has a meaning others won't see. And I, tired out and on the point of abandoning my work, once again bring my eyes close to the lens and continue. For that lonely Cross is calling for a pair of shoulders to bear it."[40]

With your good behavior, without any fuss, with all naturalness, you are setting an example. After some time, the situation in the workplace has improved. Thus, the call of St. Josemaría has been fulfilled: "To sanctify work, to sanctify yourself in work, and to sanctify others through work."[41]

---

[40] Ibid., no. 277.
[41] *Conversations with Msgr. Escrivá de Balaguer* (Manila: Sinag-tala Publishers, 1972), 14.

8

A VERY IMPORTANT VISIT

Happily, the time to go home has now come. Recalling that our Lord came to you in Holy Communion during the Holy Mass in the morning, you deem it appropriate to return that visit by going to the Blessed Sacrament at some other moment of the day, perhaps on your way home. It is a way of giving thanks to the veiled Lover. Maybe there is a church or adoration chapel on your way. A little research on this matter will facilitate things. Perhaps there is a chapel of a Catholic school or a hospital where the Eucharistic Lord is waiting for you in the tabernacle. He is there fulfilling what He promised on the day of His Ascension into Heaven: "Lo, I am with you always, to the close of the age" (Matt. 28:20).

He is always there: patient, silent, and waiting for some attention. St. Josemaría tells us, "When you approach the tabernacle, remember that He has been waiting for you for twenty centuries."[42] Since He instituted the Eucharist, He has wanted to share His life with ours.

He is a veiled Lover; the veil on the tabernacle is a reminder of this fact. He is there giving us a striking and permanent proof of His immense love, which calls for reciprocation. This visit does not require much time. In addition to your spontaneous prayers, you might choose to say three times each the Our Father, the Hail

[42] *The Way*, no. 537.

Mary, and the Glory Be. At the end, make a Spiritual Communion such as this one, which St. Josemaría learned when he was preparing for his first Communion: "I wish, Lord, to receive You with the purity, humility, and devotion with which Your most holy Mother received You, with the spirit and fervor of the saints." It is a sterling prayer that can be said anytime, anywhere. There are also occasions on which we are particularly prompted to make a Spiritual Communion, such as, for instance, when we pass in front of a Catholic church, school, or hospital, or any place where we know our Lord is in a tabernacle. There are many opportunities to give the veiled Lover some consolation.

As St. Josemaría observes, "The frequency of our visits to the Lord is in proportion to two factors: faith and the involvement of the heart; seeing the truth and loving it."[43] Jesus has remained in the Sacred Host for us so as to stay by our sides, to sustain us, to guide us. And love can be repaid only with love.

How could we not turn to the Blessed Sacrament each day, even if it is only for a few minutes, "to bring Him our greetings and our love as children and as brothers?"[44]

In many cases, even if we have a busy daily schedule, we can make a visit to the "Prisoner of Love," and it will do wonders for our spiritual lives. The reason is clear: we behave much better when we are conscious of the presence, the glance, the company, and the love of Christ.

[43] *Furrow*, no. 818.
[44] Ibid., no. 686.

9

SANCTIFYING HOME LIFE

Arriving home is a delight. Those you love so much and for whom you have been toiling all day long are waiting for your arrival. Many times throughout the day, you have been entrusting them to the silent Lord and to others in His entourage: "Lord, I pray for Pete, who is taking an exam today, and for Agnes, who is applying for a job this afternoon." Now they are all here, and you are going to give yourself to them, even though you are very tired. You will still volunteer to go out to buy medicine for the one who is coughing or to repair an appliance that is not functioning well. You realize, of course, that there is no reason why you should feel and act like a hero for doing these small things. But you know that if you do them with, and for, the love of the veiled Witness of your life, they become incredibly valuable, for they acquire the merit of love. And if you persevere in doing them this way, they will end up sanctifying you.

Perhaps, you are reading the newspaper and the youngest kid approaches you and asks you a barrage of questions; or perhaps he wants to tell you everything that happened at school. If you were to set the newspaper aside and attend to these trifles, it might be written in your book of life as something very positive, and the great Proctor will be very pleased.

You have built an atmosphere of trust at home. You see to it that your kids are not so afraid of you that they think they need to have recourse to lying when they do something wrong. They could own the lyrics of the old song "Oh, My Papa," and say about you: "He always understood." They may find you demanding, yes, but consistently reasonable and considerate. Above all, they perceive you as approachable. You are not overly afraid of losing your authority over your children. They can speak to you as a friend about everything, even intimate and personal matters, such as "crushes" they might experience.

You love sharing activities with the members of your family. You enjoy doing with your kids some of the hobbies they like. You know how to laugh with them, and you are interested in their studies and other concerns.

In our time, when people seem to be permanently immersed in their electronic gadgets — computers, cell phones, or tablets — you make it a point to organize excursions, walks, and get-togethers in order to foster true family life. Such activities are opportunities to impart formative values in an enjoyable and natural way, not so much by what you say but by what your kids see you do. For instance, they see you saying a short prayer upon starting the trip, saying grace before and after meals and, maybe, the Holy Rosary when the length of the trip calls for it. Furthermore, they see you driving well — not losing your composure in a tight spot, always cheerful, optimistic, and with good humor.

Javier Abad and Eugenio Fenoy put it well:

> Family get-togethers offer many opportunities for everyone to better know, understand and love each other. It is a time to talk about small victories, of one's dreams, of taking interest in the others and becoming aware of each one's personality; it is a time to know how to adjust to each one's quirks. If parents know how to observe their children in these moments, they will be able to draw many accurate and effective educational approaches.

The get-together cannot be the time to read the news-paper, watch television or to clean the kitchen. Neither is it the time to scold someone, or to ask him to make a public account of his studies. It is the time to show affection and to crack a joke. It is the time to laugh together.[45]

One thing you might be inclined to do, but which is better not to do, is to compare one child with another sibling or a classmate. The reason you should avoid this is simple: God has made a very unequal distribution of gifts, and each one is called, in the great test and game of life, to play with the talents he has received — that is, with the set of cards the Lord has put in his hands. Comparisons are often not only odious but out of order or even senseless. Accordingly, help your children not to compete with anybody except themselves. Thus, while encouraging each one to strive hard to be better every day, you discourage rivalry and contention.

You see to it that your home is bright and cheerful — that is, clean, simple, tidy, pleasant, warm, and very welcoming. In this way, everyone in the family loves to be in it. You are convinced that dirtiness, a lack of aesthetic sense, and bad taste are not to be taken as indicators of the virtue of poverty. You have made sure, however, that nothing extravagant or ostentatious is found in your home. You have adopted the policy of taking away useless things, and you have seen to it that all appliances, instruments, and tools are always in working condition.

You have placed around the house some nice-looking religious items, such as crucifixes and pictures of our Lady, which discreetly preside over your family life and serve as reminders to live the presence of God. Their number, however, is not excessive; you

[45] Javier Abad and Eugenio Fenoy, *Children: Their Training, Formation and Education* (Manila: Sinag-tala Publishers, 1995), 36.

do not want your home to resemble a shop of religious objects. In so doing, you have arranged your house as a Christian home characterized by simplicity.

Furthermore, you have fostered in your family an atmosphere of work without excessive stress. Everybody has his tasks to accomplish. A sample of such a situation is well-described in J. Lopez Navarro's book *The Joys and Travails of a Large Family*:

> The eldest, who is ten years old, makes two beds in the morning before going to school. The eight-year-old girl makes two beds. The seven-year-old boy goes for milk and bread. The five-year-old girl only knows enough to dress herself, but she has to have her hair combed like the other two older ones. They gulp down their breakfast because the bus never waits for the slow ones. At noon, the two elder girls set the table, but have no time to clear it. In the afternoon, the eldest prepares snacks for all the kids. The eight-year-old sets the table for dinner because the eldest is not yet through with her studies by that time.

In this manner, your family, more so if it is numerous, has become a wonderful school of human and Christian virtues such as: dedication, loyalty, generosity, industriousness, service, and order.

10

OUR LADY'S CHOICE (THE HOLY ROSARY)

Now that the whole family has gathered, it is an excellent time to pray the Holy Rosary together. It is a prayer that our Mother in Heaven likes very much. In Lourdes, where her apparitions were endorsed by many miracles, and in Fatima, where the fulfillment of several prophecies stand as guarantors, she requested that the Rosary be prayed daily. This preference of hers should always prevail over our own. Moreover, pope after pope has advised us to pray the Rosary and have enriched it with many indulgences. If the Holy Rosary is prayed as a group, a plenary indulgence may be gained.

It is useful to pause for a few seconds to contemplate each mystery and to offer each one for a different intention. Something like: one decade for the Holy Father; one for my husband; one for Uncle Bob, who is suffering from cancer; one for Louie, who is taking an exam today; one for Agnes, who is studying to pass the board; and so on.

Some people may have to rethink their opinions about praying the Holy Rosary, like a gentleman I came to know. He was a regular guy who excelled in sports in his younger days and was seeing me for spiritual direction once a week. He was making remarkable progress in his spiritual life.

I suggested that he start praying the Holy Rosary every day, and he surprised me with these words, "No, Father. I won't do that! When I was a young man, my mother forced me to pray the Rosary, and I did not like it at all. So, now that she has passed away, I won't do it."

I paused for a while, trying to recover from my shock, and told him, "I can see that you have developed a deep dislike for this prayer, when in fact it is beautiful, Gospel based, and centered in Christ, not just in Mary."

He nonetheless replied that he found it repetitious and monotonous. I mentioned to him what St. Josemaría wrote,

> Do you want to love our Lady? Well then, get to know her. How? By praying her Rosary well.
>
> But in the Rosary ... we always say the same things! Always the same?
>
> And don't people in love always say the same things to each other ...? Might it not be that you find the Rosary monotonous because, instead of pronouncing words like a man, you mumble noises while your mind is very far from God? Moreover, listen: before each decade we are told the mystery to be *contemplated*. Have you ever *contemplated* these mysteries?[46]

Furthermore, I advised him to offer each decade for a different intention; for instance, the first mystery for the Holy Father, the second for his family, the third for priests, the fourth for a relative who needs much help, and so on. Nevertheless, he replied that he just did not like this prayer.

It sounded as if this was going to be the end of our exchange of ideas regarding the Holy Rosary. It then occurred to me — it must have been an inspiration from the Holy Spirit — to tell him that

---

[46] Josemaría Escrivá, introduction to *Holy Rosary* (Manila: Sinag-tala Publishers, 2000).

obviously he disliked it, but our Lady happens to like it very much. He looked at me intently and asked, "How do you know this?"

After a few seconds, I told him: "Have you heard of Lourdes? There, in 1858, our Lady told St. Bernadette Soubirous to pray the Rosary, and at the grotto of Massabielle, our Lady was moving the beads with her fingers. Moreover, in Fatima, in 1917, our Lady told the little shepherds Lucia, Jacinta, and Francisco to pray the Holy Rosary every day. She told them this in every one of the six apparitions that happened from May through October. And these," I added, "are apparitions fully endorsed by the popes and other authorities of the Church." My friend said nothing. The next time we met, however, he was sporting a big smile on his face, and he said, "Father, I am praying the Rosary every day. It is not so hard!"

I was very happy with this turn of events. And not surprisingly, this friend of mine eventually joined Opus Dei and was very faithful and grateful until his holy death. He came to understand, wholeheartedly agreed with, and made his own these words from the end of St. Josemaría's book *Holy Rosary*:

> My friend: I have told you just a part of my secret. It is up to you, with God's help, to discover the rest. Take courage. Be faithful.
>
> Become little. Our Lord hides from the proud and reveals the treasures of his grace to the humble.
>
> Don't worry if, when thinking on your own, daring and childish words and affections arise in your heart. This is what Jesus wants, and Mary is encouraging you. If you say the Rosary in this way, you will learn to pray well.

The Holy Rosary is, in fact, solidly based on Sacred Scripture, being made up of many words from the sacred texts. It is a summary of the most important events in the life of our Savior and, if prayed well, is a source of many graces. It is a ladder, said Pope Paul VI, which you climb together with others, stair by stair, ever getting closer to the encounter with Christ. It is a practice that brings us to Christ through the Virgin Mary. It resembles the choirs of angels in Heaven, who never tires of saying the self-same, "Holy, holy, holy," and the words of our Lord in Gethsemane, who, "being in agony, prayed longer saying the self-same words" (see Luke 22:44).

The renowned American writer Msgr. Leo Trese mentioned these remembrances of his youth:

> There is the memory of Dad, leading the family Rosary. I do not know why the big base-burner in the living room should constantly intrude itself into this image from the past; but there we knelt, stooped over our chairs, while the blue anthracite flames flickered through the windows of the stove. And religion became forever a manly thing, as quiet, hardworking Dad, told the mysteries and led the beads.

There are, of course, different ways of praying the Rosary. Many, for instance, prefer to walk while reciting the prayers, in order to keep their brains active and alert. What matters most is truly to communicate with the supernatural world, in an exercise of faith and love. Pope St. John XXIII is said to have remarked in that regard, "There are different kinds of rosaries: dawn rosaries and evening rosaries, alert rosaries and sleepy rosaries, but the worst kind of all is the one that is not prayed."

Pope Paul VI said:

> Your rosary is a stairway, you ascend it together, step by step, approaching our Lady, which means approaching Christ. This is one of the characteristics of the rosary, the most important and the most beautiful of all: it is a devotion which leads us to Christ through His Blessed Mother. Christ is the

goal of this lengthy and repeated invocation of Mary. We speak to Mary so as to reach Christ. She brought Him into the world; she is the mother of the Lord. And she brings us to Him if we are devoted to her.[47]

---

[47] Paul VI, discourse, October 10, 1964.

11

SPIRITUAL READING

Continuing with our daily adventure, the day is now far advanced, and if you have not done it earlier in the day (which it is very often the best thing to do), you might still want to do something very important for your soul.

It is something that could be done at home, although at times also at work, outside office hours. It consists in reading from the New Testament for a few minutes and from another spiritual book, for about fifteen minutes in all.

This practice constitutes another contact with the invisible supernatural world, for the Holy Spirit is the principal Author of the Bible. St. Josemaría gives this advice concerning the practice of reading the Gospels: "If you wish to get close to our Lord through the pages of the Gospels, I always recommend that you try to enter in on the scene taking part as just one more person there."[48]

It is much better to read only a few lines of the New Testament intensely — that is, trying to get some message out of it — than to read many pages without being able to tell what we have read afterward.

If the other book for spiritual reading — aside from the New Testament — is well chosen, it will contain some sparks of the Light

---

[48] Josemaría Escrivá, *Friends of God* (Manila: Sinag-tala Publishers, 2000), no. 222.

emanating from the concealed Truth. A well-chosen book is one that is faithful to the teachings of the Church (the Magisterium) and is suitable for our spiritual lives. Such a book will likely be recommended or approved by our spiritual directors.

Now, books land in a home in a variety of ways: they may be purchases or gifts or lent by a friend, and so forth. It is not a matter of reading anything available, but what is truly helpful for our spiritual growth and will enable us to help others in their spiritual challenges.

It is important to devote time to spiritual reading. If prayer is the flame of the sanctuary lamp, as explained by St. Francis de Sales, then spiritual reading is the oil that feeds it. Referring to the practice of meditation, Eugene Boylan observes, "One reason why so many fail at mental prayer is that they are trying to make a fire without fuel—they have given up regular spiritual reading."[49] And St. Josemaría tells us, "By reading ... I build up a store of fuel. It seems a lifeless pile, but I often find that my mind spontaneously draws from it material which fills my prayer with life and inflames my thanksgiving after communion."[50]

St. Josemaría adds, "Don't neglect spiritual reading. Reading has made many saints."[51] This statement holds a great truth. Unfortunately, however, it is also true that reading has confused and distorted the minds of people who read books indiscriminately. For this reason he added, "Don't buy them without the advice from a Catholic who has real knowledge and discernment. It's so easy to buy something useless or harmful. How often a man thinks he is carrying a book under his arm, and it turns out to be a load of trash!"[52]

---

[49] Eugene Boylan, O.C.R., *The Spiritual Life of the Priest* (Westminster, MD: Newman Press, 1961), 17.
[50] Ibid., no. 213.
[51] *The Way*, no. 116.
[52] Ibid., no. 339.

We get news and all kinds of information in abundance from different sources. We are bombarded with commercial messages all the time. In contrast, we very seldom hear anything about God and supernatural realities. Our minds need to be nourished with something better than earthly things. We need a few minutes of spiritual reading every day, for "man does not live on bread alone" (see Matt. 4:4).

> Naturally, to be careful about selecting books for reading is perfectly compatible with having interest in the culture. The Christian affirms that the same author must have a hunger to know. Everything, from the most abstract knowledge to manual techniques, can and should lead to God. For there is no human undertaking that cannot be sanctified, that cannot be an opportunity to sanctify ourselves and to cooperate with God in the sanctification of the people with whom we work. The light of the followers of Jesus Christ should not be hidden in the depths of some valley, but should be placed on the mountain peak, so that "they may see your good works and give glory to your Father who is in heaven." [Matt. 5:16][53]

In other words, spiritual reading is important not only for our own spiritual development, but also for the help we are to give to those we manage to reach in our apostolic efforts. The love of our neighbor, which stems from our love of God, impels us to be capable of enlightening the minds and enkindling the hearts of those near us with the light of the Gospel, and no one can give what he does not have.

In our spiritual lives and in our apostolates, we need to form and address the mind, the will, and the heart. This is why we should

[53] Escrivá, *Christ Is Passing By*, no. 10.

read sound spiritual books that belong to these different categories. It might be good to alternate them. For instance, after reading a doctrinal book, such as the *Compendium of the Catholic Church*, it would be ideal to read *Friends of God* by St. Josemaría Escrivá, which is more ascetical in content; and afterward a book such as *Man, the Saint* by Jésus Urteaga, written with youthful passion; or *Jesus as Friend* by Salvatore Canals, which has a very serene prose with much spiritual drive. Depending on our circumstances, we will need books that largely address the mind or the will.

Debunking the idea that the Church is needlessly "afraid" of ideas—that all philosophical and moral positions are essentially harmless—the well-known Professor James Stenson explains:

> To the Church, a person's loss of grace, along with the faith that might lead him back to it, is an unimaginably tragic disaster. No physical calamity, no merely temporal suffering can compare with this loss....
>
> The Church has seen, time and again in history, that ideas can have profound and far reaching consequences. It has witnessed how doctrines contrary to Christian belief have led to people's personal misery and even to social catastrophe.... For generations, the Church has seen people embrace doctrinal aberrations to rationalize and justify their appetites, especially in sexual morality and the drive for power.[54]

We should, therefore, learn how to choose the books we read by paying attention to our mother, the Church. For our benefit and guidance, she gives ecclesiastical approvals, the *nihil obstat* and

---

[54] James B. Stenson, *Reading: Learning to Choose* (London: Scepter Publishers, 1984), 19–21.

the *imprimatur*, to the editions of the Bible and to other doctrinal books touching on faith and morals.

It is not always easy to be faithful to the practice of daily spiritual reading. Excuses such as lack of time or the urgency of other things seemingly more important often crop up. It is again a matter of faith. The things of God should be given priority. For that, readiness to exert the necessary effort is required. St. Josemaría has described well the usual inner struggle involved in fulfilling the plan of life:

> If you are struggling, and even more if you are really struggling, you should not be surprised at feeling tired or at times having to go against the grain, without any spiritual or human consolation. See what someone wrote to me some time ago, and which I kept for those who naively consider that grace does away with nature, "Father, for a few days now I have been feeling tremendously lazy and lacking in enthusiasm for fulfilling the plan of life. I have to force myself to do everything, and I have very little taste for it. Pray for me so that this crisis may pass, for it makes me suffer a lot to think it could make me turn from my way."
>
> I answer only: did you not know that Love demands sacrifice?[55]

It is worthwhile to conquer ourselves in order to nourish our souls with the light of the Gospel. It will give us peace and strength to face the daily challenges of life.

[55] See *Furrow*, no. 149.

12

LOOKING INSIDE OUR SOULS
WHILE FACING GOD

You are now about to end the day. Your mind turns toward the unseen World, "Where the true joys are found." First of all, you look at the nucleus of the cloud of witnesses of your life, the Triune God, and ask the Holy Spirit to illumine you in order to answer three simple questions that St. Josemaría suggests:

1. Lord, what have I done today that has displeased You?
2. What have I done that has pleased You?
3. What can I do better tomorrow?

To this effect, a specific and firm resolution will be very helpful.

The discovery of failures leads to the most important part of this brief exercise: an act of sincere *sorrow of love*. This is very different from an act of *sorrow of pride*, which is motivated by the disappointment of not seeing oneself as perfect as one would wish to be.

Venerable Fulton Sheen was fond of saying that self-examination must be done in the presence of God, for we must compare ourselves not with our neighbors, nor with our subjective ideals, but with Christ.

The examination of conscience allows us to know our strengths better, and in this way to improve our lives. It helps us to detect whatever separates us from God or affects our intimacy with Jesus Christ.

St. Josemaría writes, "Examination of conscience. A daily task. Book keeping—never neglected by anyone in business. And is there any business worth more than that of eternal life?"[56]

The realization of good things done during the day should not be a reason to be complacent; rather, it should be a motive to offer thanksgiving to the Almighty, without whom we can do nothing.

This is a well-known truism of Thales of Miletus: "The most difficult thing is to know oneself; the easiest is to criticize others."

If we do the examination of conscience well, we will obtain from the Lord self-knowledge, contrition for our sins, abandonment in God's will, and resolutions. We will avoid falling into lukewarmness this way.

The setting of one or two goals for the following day, which could be written down, is very helpful in our quest to improve in our daily struggles and move ahead in our attempts to reach the sanctity to which we are all called, as St. Josemaría Escrivá emphasized in his preaching since 1928, and which Vatican II solemnly proclaimed in 1965.

This brief examination of conscience is a good preparation for the sacrament of Reconciliation, which we need to receive immediately if we commit a mortal sin, and on a regular basis—weekly, fortnightly, or at least monthly—in order to make swift progress in our spiritual life.

[56] *The Way*, no. 235.

13

CALLING IT A DAY

Finally, it is time to rest. Still, before that, a lifting of the mind and heart to the silent supernatural world comes in handy in the form of three Hail Marys, asking Our Lady for holy purity, for ourselves and for everybody else. The very last thing that could be done is to make the Sign of the Cross and to sprinkle a couple of drops of holy water on the bed to drive Satan away. St. Teresa of Jesus affirmed: "I know by frequent experience that there is nothing which puts the devil to flight like holy water."[57]

Looking back at the day that has passed, we see that with God's help, it has been a happy day lived with both feet well grounded on this earth and yet ever in touch with the supernatural Audience. It has been, therefore, a great day, a day worth living!

As a whole, it has been a day inspired by pieces of advice mostly coming from St. Josemaría Escrivá, the founder of Opus Dei. Definitely, it has been a joyful day, lived while holding dual citizenship in heaven and on earth, loving passionately the concealed Friend and also ardently loving the world.

---

[57] *The Life of Teresa of Jesus: The Autobiography of Teresa of Ávila*, trans. and ed. E. Allison Peers (New York: Doubleday-Image Book, 1960), 198.

14

SOMETHING FOR EVERY
DAY OF THE WEEK

As St. Josemaría suggested, our contact with the invisible Audience could be very well seasoned if we place a particular emphasis on each day of the week. For instance, on Mondays, it would be a good idea to remember often the blessed souls in Purgatory. They certainly belong to the silent realm beyond the *barrier* that separates us from the *other side*. They are blessed, however, for the grace of God is with them. They are becoming more and more inflamed with the love of God and in union with Him, and they can interact with us, thanks to the Communion of Saints, which includes communication.

Accordingly, when we pass in front of a cemetery, when we read an obituary, or when we see a funeral procession, it would occur to us spontaneously to say a prayer for "My good friends, the souls in purgatory."[58]

I recall asking someone, who was quite a joker, what he does when he passes by a cemetery. His answer was quick: "Well, I just press down the accelerator!"

We certainly could do better than that, by saying a short prayer such as: "Lord, grant them eternal life! May they rest in peace!"

---

[58] See *The Way*, no. 571.

Above all, it would be an excellent idea to remember these *friends of ours*, the souls in Purgatory, in our times of prayer and at the Holy Mass, which is always offered "for the living *and the dead*."

Tuesdays, on the other hand, could be especially devoted to fostering a close relationship with our guardian angels. Perhaps, you would like to call your guardian angel fondly with some name. It might help you to address him trustfully. It is in line with what St. Josemaría tells us: "Have confidence in your Guardian Angel. Treat him as a very dear friend—that's what he is—and he will do a thousand services for you in the ordinary affairs of each day."[59] And he adds, "If you would remember the presence of your Guardian Angel and those of your neighbors, you would avoid many of the foolish things you let slip into your conversation."[60]

Moreover, on this same day, you might want to remember more often that powerful angelic protector the Lord has given us, as we take the test of our earthly sojourn, in order to counteract the diabolical influence felt in our midst. It may help you to say the St. Michael Prayer.

St. Michael Prayer

St. Michael the Archangel, defend us in battle. Be our defense against the wickedness and snares of the devil. May God rebuke him, we humbly pray; and do you, O Prince of the heavenly hosts, by the power of God, thrust into hell Satan, and all the evil spirits, who prowl about the world seeking the ruin of souls. Amen.

You may also want to say more often the Guardian Angel Prayer you might have learned when you were a little kid:

[59] Ibid., no. 562.
[60] Ibid., no. 564.

Something for Every Day of the Week

Guardian Angel Prayer

Angel of God, my guardian dear,
To whom His love commits me here,
Ever this day [or: night] be at my side,
To light and guard, to rule and guide. Amen.

Wednesdays could be the days on which we try to communicate more often and more intensely with St. Joseph. He is not only the faithful foster father of our Lord Jesus Christ, the virginal spouse of the Virgin Mary, and the prudent head and provider of the lovely household of Nazareth but is also the model of workers, the master of prayer and the interior life, the patron of the dying (for he was, most likely, fortunate enough to have Jesus and Mary at his side at the moment of his death), and also the patron of the universal Church.

By this last title, we are reminded that St. Joseph is linked personally and truly with each human being. He belongs to the *silent and supernatural world*. But this does not mean that he is like a ghost. No, he is very real, and he is interested in all of us, for Jesus — whom he helped in His redemptive work — shed His Blood for all mankind. He is truly a most loving father to everyone. This is how St. Josemaría puts it: "St. Joseph, a father to Christ, is also your father and your lord. Have recourse to him."[61]

Also on Wednesdays, we could make it a point to invoke St. Joseph in all our needs. At prayer time, we could address him confidently, paying special attention to him. In addition, we could ask him to teach us how to communicate properly with our Lord and our Blessed Mother.

Thursdays are forever linked to the Holy Eucharist, for it was on a Thursday that our Lord, during the Last Supper, instituted

---

[61] *The Way*, no. 559.

it. It might be a good idea to devote this day to meditating and conversing with the Persons of the veiled Audience about this great mystery of faith.

This is how St. Matthew, inspired by the Holy Spirit, recorded for us the institution of the Eucharist:

> Now as they were eating, Jesus took bread, and blessed, and broke it, and gave it to the disciples and said, "Take, eat; this is my body." And he took a cup, and when he had given thanks he gave it to them, saying, "Drink of it, all of you; for this is my blood of the covenant, which is poured out for many for the forgiveness of sins. (Matt. 26:26–28)

It was the farewell supper that linked the old and the new covenants, in order that the following day would be sealed on the Cross, with the precious blood of our Lord. It is appropriate, therefore, to do all we can to make every Thursday a Eucharistic day. We could begin by attending Holy Mass, even if we are not yet able to do so on the other weekdays. It is a great thing to be present at the re-presentation of the sacrifice of Calvary and to receive worthily the Bread of Life on a day that is not a holy day of obligation. Under these circumstances, we enjoy the additional and personal assurance that we attend the Holy Mass not out of any fear or requirement but out of pure and free love.

On Thursdays, we could make it a point to bring to our prayer this great mystery of love and not to fail in visiting our Lord in the Blessed Sacrament, the silent, and often lonely Guest of countless Catholic churches and chapels.

In addition, we could endeavor to multiply the expression of our eagerness to receive Him sacramentally, by reciting Spiritual Communions throughout the day. Many have found it helpful to use one that St. Josemaría liked and recommended: "I wish, Lord, to receive You with the purity, humility, and devotion with which your most holy Mother received you, with the spirit and fervor of the saints."

On Fridays, the memory of Mount Calvary looms high. It was on a Friday when Jesus was hung on a cross for our salvation. It would be a great pity if we were so immersed in our earthly pursuits that such remembrance would not mean anything to us. Therefore, we will do well to make an effort to recall it throughout the day. Without doubt, the best moment for that will be in the Sacrifice of the Mass that we attend. There we find ourselves at Golgotha, with the same High Priest, the same Victim, and the same intention Jesus Christ had at that time. This is possible because He, the eternal Logos (the Second Person of the Blessed Trinity), always lives—as God—in eternity, that is, outside the constraints of time and space.

If it is compatible with our professional and family duties, it would be an excellent thing to recite on Fridays the Way of the Cross, a practice that our Mother the Church has enriched with generous indulgences. This is how St. Josemaría puts it: "The Way of the Cross. Here indeed is a strong and fruitful devotion! May you make it a habit to go over those fourteen points of our Lord's Passion and Death each Friday. I assure you that you'll gain strength for the whole week."[62]

To that, Blessed Alvaro del Portillo added, "The Way of the Cross is not a sad devotion. Msgr. Escrivá taught many times that Christian joy has its roots in the shape of a cross. If the Passion of Christ is a way of pain, it is also a path of hope leading to certain victory."[63]

Saturdays have always been linked to our Blessed Mother, Mary. Christians have not forgotten that sorrowful Saturday when the

---

[62] *The Way*, no. 556.

[63] Alvaro del Portillo, foreword to *The Way of the Cross*, by Josemaría Escrivá (London: Scepter Press, 1982), 13.

body of Jesus Christ lay in the tomb, and Mary inspired the disciples with confidence and provided them with the great support of her unshakable faith. At the darkest hour, Mary was truly the hope of the Christians. For this reason, over the centuries, Saturday has been a day devoted to our Lady.

It would be an excellent idea to make every Saturday a Marian day. We could begin by paying special attention to our Lady when we make our Morning Offering and address the Triune God and His entourage. She is the Queen of Heaven — that is, the most important person in our Lord's retinue. After God comes Mary, and she deserves our special attention. Accordingly, after offering our entire day to the Almighty, we might want to speak filially to the Virgin Mary, asking her protection during the day.

There is a very well-known ancient prayer, the Memorare, that Christians have prayed countless times, and it comes to us from St. Bernard of Clairvaux (1090–1153), a Doctor of the Church, who was very much in love with Mary. It would be a good thing to say it often on Saturdays:

Memorare

Remember, O most gracious Virgin Mary, that never was it known that anyone who fled to your protection, implored your help, or sought your intercession was left unaided. Inspired by this confidence, I fly unto you, O Virgin of virgins, my Mother. To you I come, before you I stand, sinful and sorrowful. O Mother of the Word Incarnate, despise not my petitions, but, in your mercy, hear and answer me. Amen.

In addition, since Saturdays are devoted to Our Lady, it would be fitting to pray with more intensity all our Marian devotions, such as the Holy Rosary.

This is what Pope Pius XII said about it:

What a sweet and most pleasing spectacle to God when, at eventide, the Christian home resounds with repeated praises in honor of the august Queen of heaven! Then the recitation of the Rosary reunites the parents and their children who return from their daily work and brings them together before the image of the Virgin in an admirable union of hearts. It unites them piously with those absent and with the dead.[64]

Furthermore, Pope St. John XXIII called it "a very commendable form of prayer and meditation."[65] The popes have wholeheartedly recommended the Holy Rosary and have enriched it with indulgences.

It is also very appropriate to recite or sing a Hail Holy Queen every Saturday in our Lady's honor. It is a very beautiful ancient prayer that surely pleases our Blessed Mother. As in the Hail Mary, we remind the Virgin Mary of her splendid titles, most especially of her condition as Queen, and we end humbly, asking her help for us who are still "in this our exile." It is a prayer that is bound to touch her Immaculate Heart.

Hail Holy Queen

Hail, Holy Queen, Mother of mercy, our life, our sweetness, and our hope. To you do we cry, poor banished children of Eve. To you do we send up our sighs, mourning, and weeping in this valley of tears. Turn, then, most gracious advocate, your eyes of mercy toward us, and after this, our exile, show unto us the blessed fruit of your womb, Jesus. O clement, O loving, O sweet Virgin Mary.

[64] Pius XII, Encyclical *Ad Apostolorum Principis* (June 29, 1958), no. 10.

[65] John XXIII, Encyclical on the Rosary *Grata Recordatio* (September 26, 1959), no. 2.

Through Sr. Lucia of Fatima, our Lady has also requested that we observe with particular devotion the first Saturday of five consecutive months: attending Holy Mass, receiving Communion worthily in reparation for sins, praying the Rosary in honor of her Immaculate Heart, and spending at least fifteen minutes meditating on the mysteries of the Rosary. It might be a good idea to live this devotion every first Saturday of the month.

In line with this request, which comes from our Lady herself, it would be a praiseworthy resolution to dedicate every first Saturday to live and propagate among our friends a love for the Immaculate Heart of Mary and to offer atonement for the sins that are committed all over the world.

Finally, in addition to the weekly commemoration of the Resurrection of our Lord, we could devote Sundays to honoring, in a special way, the Blessed Trinity, which is at the very core and summit of the *Company of Witnesses* of our lives. The *Catechism of the Catholic Church* calls the mystery of the Most Holy Trinity "the central mystery of the Christian faith and life" (234).

This great mystery should occupy first place not only at the speculative level but also at the practical level in the lives of Christians. A good contribution to this is making every Sunday a special *Trinitarian day*.

On Sundays, whenever we make the Sign of the Cross, we could strive to do it in such a way that we really mean what we are saying: "In the name of the Father, and of the Son, and of the Holy Spirit!" Furthermore, we could bring to our mental prayer this great mystery of our Faith, taking it as the topic of meditation for a few minutes and, perhaps, occasionally, we might find it useful to use the words of the Te Deum, the Angelic Trisagion, or the Athanasian Creed.[66]

---

[66] These prayers are included in the suggested prayers at the end of this book.

On Sundays, while going from one occupation to another, we might find it helpful to repeat some aspiration; for instance: "Glory be to the Father, to the Son, and to the Holy Spirit!" or this one that St. Josemaría said and recommended a great deal: "Hail Mary, daughter of God the Father, Hail Mary, mother of God the Son, Hail Mary, spouse of God the Holy Spirit! Greater than you, none but God!"[67]

---

[67] *The Way*, no. 496.

15

FREQUENT CONFESSION

Among the practices recommended by the unanimous and constant Catholic Tradition, the sacrament of Reconciliation holds pride of place. Saints, Doctors of the Church, popes, and bishops have always advised the frequent reception of this sacrament. Furthermore, those who have founded new institutions within the Church for the purpose of promoting, among other goals, the sanctification of its members, have persistently established the weekly—or at least very frequent—reception of this sacrament of joy and peace we call Confession. The reason is clear: it was established by Jesus Christ as a sacrament, a channel of grace and of reconciliation with God and the Church, and a powerful means for spiritual growth.

Confession is there not only to forgive sins and give sanctifying grace if it was lost but also to increase this grace. It is instrumental in helping and enriching the soul in the form of sacramental grace and actual graces that allow us to have more strength to overcome temptations and strive for virtue. Confession makes us humbler. It is, therefore, a great means for spiritual progress. In consequence, the more a soul desires to be united to God, the more it wishes to receive the sacrament of Penance. This sacrament is wholly necessary for the forgiveness of grave sins. The act of perfect contrition forgives mortal sins only if it is accompanied by a desire to receive the sacrament of Reconciliation.

The precept of going to Confession once a year, if we had any mortal sin, is a mere *minimum*. It aims to ensure that we do not despise the opportunity of reconciliation that Jesus Christ offers to us through His Church. But if we take seriously the words of Sacred Scripture, which are addressed to everyone: "This is the will of God, your sanctification" (1 Thess. 4:3), then the need for more frequent Confession becomes crystal clear.

Some people are hesitant to go to Confession, for they feel that their sins are too many and too grievous. They are to bear in mind this passage from St. Luke:

> And the Pharisees and their scribes murmured against his disciples, saying, "Why do you eat and drink with tax collectors and sinners?" And Jesus answered them, "Those who are well have no need of a physician, but those who are sick; I have not come to call the righteous, but sinners to repentance." (Luke 5:30–32)

Our Lord is "rich in mercy" to an amazing degree. St. Josemaría puts it this way:

> Consider what depths of mercy lie in the Justice of God! For, according to human justice, he who pleads guilty is punished, but in the divine court, he is pardoned. Blessed be the holy sacrament of Penance![68]

Moreover, in order to stress this point, Jesus Himself said, "I tell you, there will be more joy in heaven over one sinner who repents than over ninety-nine righteous persons who need no repentance" (Luke 15:7). This text shows how grateful we should be for His immense mercy every time we receive the sacrament of Reconciliation.

---

[68] *The Way*, no. 309.

In Confession, it is essential to be repentant for having committed sins. It is not enough to regret having done something wrong or to be eager to leave its memory behind. We ought to be truly determined not to do it anymore. Moreover, the reason for this repentance should be the love of God. He is the one who is most seriously offended. Emotional sensations and tears are welcome, if sincere, but they are not at all necessary.

Aside from the immense supernatural advantages of frequent Confession, there are a number of human returns. Raphael Bonelli, an Austrian psychiatrist, says:

> Normally, a person who confesses regularly obtains a high knowledge of himself, or herself. The reason is that he or she develops the capacity to question himself, or herself, and to pass judgment on his or her emotions, feelings, passions, and actions. Such a person acquires the aptitude to prioritize the power of reflection over a passing sensation, and does not perceive his or her own actions as events bound to destiny, but as something to submit to a rational judgment. This leads to a healthy consciousness of oneself, rooted in one's condition as a son or daughter of God. Ultimately, it translates itself into an attitude of deep gratitude to a merciful God, who forgives sins. Such persons are able to forgive more easily other individuals who have injured them. Moreover, they live more peacefully and more cheerfully.[69]

---

[69] Raphael Bonelli, *Palabra* (Madrid: Ediciones Palabra, July 2012), no. 589.

16

SPIRITUAL GUIDANCE

Spiritual direction stands side by side with frequent Confession. In line with the entire Catholic Tradition, St. Josemaría recommends it wholeheartedly:

> It's good for you to know this doctrine, which is always sound: your own spirit is a bad advisor, a poor pilot to steer your soul through the squalls and storms and across the reefs of the interior life.
>
> That's why it is the Will of God that the command of the ship be entrusted to a master who, with his light and knowledge, can guide us to a safe port.[70]

He further explains the need for spiritual direction, saying: "You wouldn't think of building a good house to live on earth without an architect. How can you ever hope, without a director, to build the castle of your sanctification in order to live forever in heaven?"[71]

It can also be compared to coaching in sports, for the Christian life is a supernatural test that requires training and guidance. It is a recognized fact in the world of sports that having a good coach often spells the difference between victory and defeat for a given team or player.

[70] *The Way*, no. 59.
[71] Ibid., no. 60.

Undoubtedly, the principal director of each soul is the Holy Spirit. We need to listen to Him and follow His promptings with docility. It is also His will that we obediently follow the advice given to us by His representatives, who guide us in spiritual matters and are instruments of the veiled Spirit.

Accordingly, it is wise to meditate afterward on the advice we have received in our personal prayer and to find a way to put it into practice, with the certainty that it is the will of God for us.

It is a great thing to have someone who has special help from God and to whom we can tell, with freedom, our ups and downs, our joys and sorrows, in order to receive some comfort or encouragement. Above all, it is great because it is a supernatural means, highly recommended by the Church to become closer to God.

We are to go punctually to spiritual direction with the humility of a child, with eagerness to be known as we really are, with the desire to be helped in our spiritual struggles; thus, making it easy for whoever guides our soul to demand more from us, as well as pointing out, without hesitation, whatever needs to be mentioned.

It follows from the considerations above that the virtue of sincerity is very important for effective spiritual direction. St. Josemaría says, "Anyone who hides a temptation from his director shares a secret with the devil. He has become a friend of the enemy."[72] And he adds: "If you are sincere with God, with your director, and your fellowmen, I shall be certain of your perseverance."[73]

Upon entrusting the direction of our souls to qualified persons, we do not in any way lose our freedom, responsibility, and initiative. This is similar to how a pilot of a commercial plane does not lack freedom when he pays much attention to what is said from the control tower. He trusts the advice given and knows that it is

[72] *Furrow*, no. 323.
[73] Ibid., no. 325.

for his own good as well as for the good of many others. No pilot thinks that his freedom is restricted by the control tower, for it is clear to him that he is in control of the plane, and that he has to assume the consequent responsibility.

17

MONTHLY DAY OF RECOLLECTION

No matter how busy we are, it is very good to take some time out once a month to further our spiritual lives. It is a matter of being with our Lord in more familiar terms than usual and to deepen our knowledge and implementation of the Christian Faith.

It is a golden opportunity to have a lengthier contact with our Lord and to examine our consciences genuinely. It is a little break from our usual daily activities, in order to be *in silence with God* and to be closer to Him. When the time for our monthly recollection comes, we are to give preference to this opportunity to be with our Lord — often facing the tabernacle — over temporal concerns.

The purpose of the day of recollection is to improve our spiritual formation and to immerse ourselves more deeply in God. Hence, it would not be right to limit ourselves to listening to a series of meditations and talks, as if they constituted an academic affair. They are not mere classes or lectures. They are supposed to help us grow in our interior lives.

It is not so much a matter of always hearing new things, in what has been termed as *neolatria* (worshipping novelty), but of digging deeper and deeper into the inexhaustible Christian message, applying it to ourselves and sharing it with others.

18

YEARLY RETREAT

As it is commonly known, it is very helpful to set aside a few days once a year to commune with God, to grow in the interior life and develop our contemplative spirit. It also helps us to review our spiritual struggles of the previous months and to come up with a few realistic resolutions.

Many recognize the importance of an annual checkup for our bodily health. Should we not value our spiritual health even more?

The retreat is dedicated entirely to our Lord. The observance of silence facilitates our inner conversation with the withdrawn God. Noise is an obstacle we are to avoid on a retreat.

A retreat provides an occasion to leave behind our daily concerns, leaving them in God's hands, and to focus our attention on the most important matters in our lives.

19

ALWAYS IN GOD'S PRESENCE

Relating with our veiled God and very loving Father is something that has to be done not only daily or weekly, but always. That is, we must maintain the *presence of God*. This consists in being aware that He is alive and looking lovingly at us. It amounts to removing the veil that covers the hidden Father. Perhaps, we recall very fondly instances in which we have perceived God's presence vividly. They are no more than subjective experiences, and thus, they lack objective value. Nevertheless, for us, for our personal pilgrimage of faith, they are very valuable.

To habitually have the presence of God, we are to slow down a bit to avoid being always too much in a hurry. We are to ponder things and give importance to what is truly important. It is equally necessary to have enough self-dominion to reject energetically frivolous thoughts and images that might invade our minds, our imaginations, and our memories. It is also important to fill our hearts with aspirations that express the supernatural love we have in our hearts — that is, to carry on a conversation with the Persons of the veiled supernatural world. All this requires that we bear ever in mind that there is, as it were, a *one-way mirror* between us and God and the other world. He sees us perfectly, but we do not see Him.

St. Josemaría writes:

THE LITTLE MANUAL FOR SPIRITUAL GROWTH

It's necessary to be convinced that God is always near us. Too often we live as though Our Lord were somewhere far off—where the stars shine. We fail to realize that He is also by our side—always.

For He is a loving Father. He loves each one of us more than all the mothers in the world can love their children, helping us, blessing ... and forgiving.[74]

When St. Josemaría was working on the documents for the canonical approvals of the Work, he had on his table a piece of green glass that had been used on an electric post as an insulator. Cables carrying electric current had been placed around it. The founder of Opus Dei reflected on this and concluded that he did not want to be an obstacle to the transmission of supernatural grace. That piece of cheap glass helped him to ask Jesus, time and again, never to be an insulator of grace, but to be a good conductor of spiritual energy. On his working table, under a round piece of crystal, he kept the following inscriptions:

Sufre, si quieres gozar.
Baja, si quieres subir.
Pierde, si quieres ganar.
Muere, si quieres vivir.

Suffer, if you want to enjoy.
Come down, if you want to go up.
Lose, if you want to win.
Die, if you want to live.

I have a small picture of the founder of Opus Dei on which, in May 1958, he wrote: *Semper ut iumentum!* (Always like a donkey!) It was an expression of his fondness for this little animal on

---

[74] *The Way*, no. 267.

account of its perseverance, hard work, austerity, and humility. He had a similar fondness for ducks, about which he said with good humor, "I like the fact that ducks learn to swim by swimming." The sight of these animals were good aids in maintaining his awareness of the presence of God.

On his working desk in a house on Diego de Leon Street in Madrid, and later in Rome, the founder of Opus Dei had a globe, which he liked to turn around to help him pray for the apostolate carried out by his daughters and sons all over the five continents.

For bookmarks, he used strips of paper with the phrase "*Ure igne Sancti Spiritus!*" (Inflame me with the fire of the Holy Spirit) written in his bold handwriting.[75] St. Josemaría made many suggestions for "human devices," such as:

> Before you start working, place a crucifix on your desk or beside the tools you work with. From time to time glance at it.... When tiredness creeps in, your eyes will go towards Jesus, and you will find new strength to continue with your task.
>
> For that crucifix is more than a picture of someone you love — parents, children, wife, sweetheart.... He is everything: your father, your brother, your friend, your God, the very love of your loves.[76]

It is the same idea conveyed in a touching point of his book *The Way*, which I quoted earlier:

> You ask me, "Why that wooden Cross?" And I quote from a letter: "As I raise my eyes from the microscope, my sight comes to rest on the Cross — black and empty. That Cross

---

[75] *The Forge*, no. 923.
[76] *The Way of the Cross*, no. 97.

without a Corpus is a symbol; it has a meaning others won't see. And I, tired out and on the point of abandoning my work, once again bring my eyes close to the lens and continue. For that lonely Cross is calling for a pair of shoulders to bear it."[77]

It is as striking as this point in *Furrow*:

You are writing to me in the kitchen, by the stove. It is early afternoon. It is cold. By your side, your youngest sister—the last one to discover the divine folly of living her Christian vocation to the full—is peeling potatoes. To all appearances, you think her work is the same as before. And yet, what a difference there is!

It is true: before she *only* peeled potatoes; now, she is sanctifying herself peeling potatoes.[78]

The Lord, who is pleased with the incense offered to Him during a solemn liturgical ceremony, is also pleased with the toil offered in countless settings in the world of labor, manual or intellectual, when it is offered as a gift to the Father, in union with the Son, with the help of the Holy Spirit. In this manner, it becomes an act of "worship" that has a co-redeeming value: through Him, with Him, and in Him!

St. Josemaría advises this for all moments:

Be convinced, my child, that God has a right to ask us: Are you thinking about me? Are you aware of me? Do you look at me as your support? Do you seek me as the Light of your life, as your shield ... as your all?

[77] *The Way*, no. 277.
[78] *Furrow*, no. 498.

Renew, then, this resolution: In times the world calls good, I will cry out: "Lord!" In times it calls bad, again I will cry: "Lord!"[79]

He adds, "Ask yourself many times during the day: Am I doing at this moment what I ought to be doing?"[80] And when things seem to go well:

"Have you seen the gratitude of little children? Imitate them, saying to Jesus when things are favorable and when they aren't, "How good you are! How good!"[81]

Lastly, as we try to find the covered God, we find Him reflected in our fellowmen; and we are guided by the Gospels, which show how Jesus identified Himself with the neighbor: "As you did it to one of the least of these my brethren, you did it to me" (Matt. 25:40).

The realization that the veiled God is our Father, who loves us more than all the most loving fathers on this earth put together is a most fundamental and consoling truth. This "sense of divine filiation" should manifest itself in a number of ways. Examples of this could be: the attentive and unhurried recitation of the Lord's Prayer, paying special attention to the words, "Our Father"; bringing to our prayer, as a frequent topic of meditation, the great truth of being adopted children of God; addressing our veiled Lord with words such as, "Hi, Daddy!"; valuing and celebrating the anniversary of our Baptism, when we became children of God and heirs of Heaven — heirs, that is, of the treasures that Jesus Christ has earned for us with His blood.

God shelters Himself only to enable us to take with all freedom the great test of faith, which is the life of each of us. Actually, He

---

[79] *The Forge*, no. 506.
[80] *The Way*, no. 772.
[81] Ibid., no. 894.

is eager to be with us; He delights being among us. He calls us and comes to us, while remaining a withdrawn Lord only for the sake of the test we are taking.

Acts of thanksgiving for the favors received from His invisible Hand should be made more frequently. Practice thanksgiving for everything, for, as St. Paul teaches, "In everything God works for good with those who love him" (Rom. 8:28). Hence, we are to be thankful for those things that are obviously good, and for those which are not so, if permitted by Him. Moreover, we are to be grateful for the many blessings we have received even though we are not aware of them.

Considering that the silent God is offended without pause all over the world, it is our duty to offer expiation for sins. We may use this prayer taught by the angel to the little shepherds of Fatima: "My God, I believe, I adore, I hope, and I love You. I ask pardon for all those who do not believe, do not adore, do not hope, and do not love You."

In a similar vein, St. Josemaría says: "Don't be so blind or so thoughtless that you fail to say at least an ejaculation to Mary Immaculate, whenever you go past a place where you know Christ is being offended."[82]

These are *acts of atonement* for the many sins committed against the Lord all over the world—sadly, an enormous number every minute. In 2011, the National Center for Victims of Crime reported that in the United States:

- One child dies from abuse or neglect every 5 hours.
- One person is murdered every 35 minutes.
- One person is robbed every 1.3 minutes.
- One person is raped or sexually assaulted every 4.2 minutes.
- One person is killed in an alcohol-related traffic accident every 48.5 minutes.

[82] See *The Way*, no. 269.

This is a partial account of the American "crime clock." It is an appalling statistical report of crimes committed every day, every hour, every minute in the United States. It is sobering to think that God, the silent Examiner, is continuously witnessing many more sins perpetrated all over the world, including many that are committed internally and are therefore undetectable to us, but are real offenses against God. We get easily distracted, but He never does; He perceives absolutely everything, and Jesus Christ paid for it on Calvary with His blood.

We are to offer some token expiation for sins, knowing that many of them are atrocious. Our desire to atone for sins should extend first to our own and then to all those committed since the beginning of mankind and to all those that will be perpetrated until the end of time — in other words, to all the offenses directed to our loving Lord in the past, present, and future. St. Josemaría says:

> We want to offer our life, our unstinting dedication, in expiation for our sins; for the sins of all men, our brothers; for the sins committed at all times, and for those that will be committed until the end of time. Above all, for the Catholics, for God's chosen ones who do not respond, those who betray the special love God our Lord has bestowed on them.
>
> To be second to none in loving; to win all souls for Christ; to offer abundant reparation for the offenses committed against the most Sacred Heart of Jesus: these are our ambitions.[83]

When the mind finds it difficult to communicate with the living God, *aspirations* come in very handy; they are the little twigs that keep the sacred fire of our life of faith alive. Aspirations, which could be compared to darts that spring from the mind and heart

---

[83] Josemaría Escrivá, Letter, January 9, 1932, 83.

and might reach the mouth, are short, simple prayers that we may compose or select. Some are spontaneous expressions of genuine love for God and the other persons of the concealed supernatural world. Others are cries for help or expressions of some other sentiment, such as "Jesus, I love you! Mary, help!" Often, these spontaneous reactions are prompted by the sight of a holy picture or a crucifix, which remind us of lofty realities. They respond to the needs of our hearts and of our human condition.

In addition, frequent, little sacrifices, acts of self-denial, or *mortifications*, offered as tokens of love for Christ crucified, could not be lacking in a person who wants to co-redeem with the Lord. There is no greater honor than to be permitted to suffer with Christ. St. Josemaría says, "Jesus suffers to carry out the will of the Father. And you, who also want to carry out the most holy will of God, following the steps of the Master, can you complain if you meet suffering on your way?"[84]

Mortification is our tool to heal the wounds inflicted in our nature by sin. By keeping the body under the control of the soul, we permit God's grace to restore the harmony that sin has managed to destroy.

Judging by the way many people react in the face of pain, they seem to have forgotten that Paradise was lost a long time ago. In this testing ground, in this exile, the veiled Examiner wants us to react properly. The founder of Opus Dei says, "In this life, we must expect the Cross. Those who do not expect the Cross are not Christians, and they will be unable to avoid their own 'cross,' which will drive them to despair."[85]

Without a Christian vision of things, suffering seems to be something weird and beyond our understanding. And yet, when

[84] *The Way*, no. 213.
[85] *The Forge*, no. 763.

considered with eyes of faith and with trust in our veiled Father, pain has meaning. It shows us God's providence. It is a means to purify us by removing the scars due to sins. When needed, it shortens or even cancels our future stay in Purgatory. It also helps us to be humble — that is, realistic — upon experiencing the limitations and the truth of our present human condition. Suffering leads us to be more understanding toward our fellow human beings and unites us more closely with Jesus Christ, giving us the opportunity to co-redeem with Him. Additionally, suffering makes us more useful and fruitful in the immense apostolate done by the Church throughout the world.

Every so often, the Cross of our Savior comes our way without our searching for it. It comes in real circumstances, not imagined ones. In other instances, though, they are not objective; we "invent" them. In both cases, we ought to take things well. We are to climb up those steps suggested by St. Josemaría: "to be resigned to the will of God; to conform to the will of God; to want the will of God; to love the will of God."[86]

In addition to accepting the passive sufferings that the veiled Proctor wishes to send us, we are to look for ways of offering Him tokens of our love in the form of little active sacrifices. These little acts of self-denial will prepare us to take well the bigger challenges we might meet in life. If we were self-indulgent, however, we would easily fail when big temptations or huge sufferings come our way. The reason is simple: we would have become, somehow, like spoiled brats.

[86] *The Way*, no. 774.

20

MORTIFICATION OF THE SENSES

Our senses are like the windows of our souls. It is through the senses that our souls get in contact with the surrounding world, and we want only good things to reach our souls. Consequently, we need to mortify each one of our senses.

First, the sense of *sight:* "Why should you look around, if you carry 'your world' within you?"[87] "The eyes! Through them much wickedness enters into the soul. How many experiences like David's! If you guard your eyes, you'll be assured of guarding your heart."[88]

We are to be on guard and control our sight, especially when using the Internet or viewing movies and videos.

We are also to exert custody over our sense of *hearing*, preventing it from receiving things incompatible with our love for God, and also avoiding, or cutting short, conversations that do not please the Lord and amount to a waste of time.

Similarly, also, our sense of *taste:* We should include "among the ingredients of our meals ... that 'most delicious' of ingredients, mortification."[89] St. Josemaría also advises us "to eat a bit less of what we like most, and a bit more of what we like less." "The body

---

[87] Ibid., no. 184.
[88] Ibid., no. 183.
[89] *The Forge*, no. 783.

must be given a little less than it needs. Otherwise it will turn traitor."[90] And we are also warned that: "Gluttony is the forerunner of impurity."[91]

We are to eat with temperance and drink alcoholic beverages with sobriety. Hence, it is better not to give the body full satisfaction in these things. It is enough to consume what is needed to keep our body healthy and efficient, and no more.

Mortification of the interior senses is also important, for, as Eugene Boylan says, "No man who always says 'yes' in his thoughts, will be able to say 'no' when it comes to action."[92] And he adds: "Day-dreaming, reveries, memories, and anticipations, should be carefully controlled."[93]

Mortification ensures that we have the right dispositions to converse with God. Without sacrifice, it is hard to converse with the veiled God in an intimate manner, or to have a calm and happy awareness of His presence. St. Josemaría affirms: "Unless you mortify yourself, you'll never be a prayerful soul."[94]

We should not allow distractions to harm our conversation with God. Some are unavoidable — it is part of being human — but others can and ought to be driven away by practicing inner mortification.

This means that we are to be in command of our imaginations. The imagination is a great gift from God, but also a liability, if not kept under control. St. Teresa of Jesus called it "the mad woman of the house," for it can build up many images in our minds that distract us from the truly real and important things. Without guarding it, we could be living in a world of fantasy, perhaps in an attempt to escape reality, and, as a result, become open to a host of temptations.

[90] *The Way*, no. 196.
[91] Ibid., no. 126.
[92] Boylan, *The Spiritual Life of the Priest*, 83.
[93] Ibid.
[94] *The Way*, no. 172.

A similar thing happens with our memory. The memory is, certainly, another valuable gift. If not checked, however, it could transport us deep into the past; foster nostalgic remembrances, useless regrets, or grudges; and arouse fresh temptations. The founder of Opus Dei writes, "Don't think any more about your fall. Besides overwhelming and crushing you under its weight, that recollection may easily be an occasion of future temptation."[95]

An area very rich in opportunities to practice mortification is the *work* in which we are engaged. In our professions or trades, in any honest occupation, we can offer our Lord many acts of self-giving by working well, with human proficiency, punctually, and in an orderly manner, all done with the desire for perfection, not for human glory, but for God's glory.

[95] Ibid., no. 262.

21

STUDY

Among the good habits that characterize a "modern apostle," is a penchant for study. It shows an eagerness and seriousness in learning. St. Josemaría Escrivá puts it this way: "If you are to serve God with your mind, to study is a grave obligation for you."[96] And he added: "Study—any professional development—is a serious obligation for us.[97] For a student, to study is a duty of justice. It is due to himself, to society, to his parents, and to his teachers. For a student, studying is a duty to himself because it consists in acquiring knowledge and skills in an orderly way so that the student might find in the future the right work to earn a living and support a family. It is a duty to society, because studying prepares the student to help others by striving to advance the common good of the society in which he lives. It is a duty to his parents, because studying hard is a way of trying—only trying—to repay what they have done for him. It is a duty to his teachers, for they devote much time imparting their knowledge to the student.

In addition, studying helps everyone to acquire personal maturity. The effort to study seriously one day after another, whether liking it or not, whether enjoying what is being studied or not,

[96] Ibid., no. 336.
[97] Ibid., no. 334.

contributes to the development of such virtues as self-mastery, diligence, patience, and order.

The founder of Opus Dei clearly saw the importance of study for character building; he wrote, "Student: form in yourself a solid and active piety; be outstanding in study; have strong desires for professional apostolate. And with that vigor in your religious and scientific training, I promise you rapid and far-reaching developments."[98]

He added: "Work! When you are engrossed in professional work, the life of your soul will improve, and you'll become more of a man for you'll get rid of that 'carping spirit' that consumes you."[99]

More importantly, study is a means of sanctification, for it can be a way of uniting ourselves to the veiled God. It can become a form of prayer: "An hour of study, for a modern apostle, is an hour of prayer."[100]

To elevate our study to the supernatural level, we should invoke the Holy Spirit and offer it to Him. Our studying, however, has to be done to the best of our ability. We should not dare to offer God a job poorly done, a sloppy task that would make people laugh.

We have to work with *constancy*, avoiding *butterflying* from one occupation to another, sticking to a well-thought-out schedule day after day; with *order*, keeping faithfully the right priorities, beginning and ending on time, and avoiding the practice of *cramming* before the tests. And, finally, we are to study with *intensity*. Concentration works wonders. We are to avoid dissipation and distractions. It is not a matter of skimming over things, but of going deeper into the material. "*Non multa, sed multum*" — not many things, but well, advises the author of *The Way*.[101]

---

[98] Ibid., no. 346.
[99] Ibid., no. 343.
[100] Ibid., no. 335.
[101] Ibid., no. 333.

Study

It will help to tell our sheltered Father that we dedicate our study to Him for some intention, such as for the Church or for a friend who needs help. And while studying, we could renew this dedication a number of times. "Then, how valuable your hour of work becomes as you persevere with the same effort a little longer, a few minutes more, until the job is finished."[102] In this way, our study—and we should love studying, even after graduation, adopting the attitude of a "perpetual student"—will be a means to sanctify this noble occupation and to strive for personal sanctification. Furthermore, it will also be a sterling means to bring others closer to God, in short, to save and to sanctify others.

St. Josemaría referred to this apostolate when he wrote: " 'Come follow me, and I will make you fishers of men.' Not without reason does our Lord use these words: men—like fish—have to be caught by the head. What an evangelical depth there is in the intellectual apostolate!"[103]

Working side by side with other colleagues affords us an opportunity to draw them to the apostolate. Well-earned professional respect and prestige provides bait, an attraction, for the *fishers of men.*

We ought to hunger for knowledge, not to impress people, but rather, as much as we can, to put all learning at the feet of Christ.

[102] *Friends of God*, no. 67.
[103] *The Way*, no. 978.

22

ORDER

Order is another important virtue that ensures that we keep our priorities: *First things first!* It prevents us from deserving the classic warning of St. Augustine: "You run well, but out of the track! You will be disqualified!" Furthermore, it multiplies our time.

St. Augustine describes order as an arrangement "of equal and unequal things, giving to each its proper place."[104]

There is an observable order in nature. The entire creation is ordained to the glory of God; but man, in order to achieve his end, has to ordain himself utilizing the freedom God has given him. Since this is not done in a single act but in a multitude of actions, he has to arrange these actions among themselves, having the end in view. Hence, for man to observe order is a duty.

Accordingly, when man fails to keep this order in relation to God, he sins. The greatest disorder, in fact, is to prefer a limited creature to the infinite Creator.

For a good action of ours to be pleasing to God, it must be ordained to its natural and supernatural goal. In this, the virtue of prudence has an essential role to play. It ordains the means to their end and, ultimately, to the fulfillment of God's plan.

---

[104] St. Augustine, *De Civitate Dei*, bk. 19, chap. 13.

It is the virtue of order that leads us to reach our ultimate goal—to fulfill God's will. Anything opposed to it is disorder.

In addition, order brings peace and serenity to our lives. Not in vain, St. Augustine calls peace "the tranquility of order."[105] Conversely, where there is disorder, there is anxiety.

Order should show itself in our ideas, in our minds. Not all our thoughts have the same importance. There ought to be a hierarchy and coordination among our ideas, and all of them are to be related to the supreme idea of God.

Thus, for instance, the truths of our Faith, as taught by the Church, are to occupy the highest place in the order of our ideas. Then come the scientific, professional, and experimental truths, and finally, at the last place, those that are simple opinions.

Order should also reign in our love and in our affections. This means that the love for God should always occupy the number-one position in our hierarchy of values; then our love for our family, both supernatural and natural, our friends and colleagues, our fellow Catholics, our fellow Christians, all our compatriots, all human beings, all creatures, and so forth.

Likewise, order should be lived in our actions.

- In the fulfillment of our daily plan of life, always placing first things first, we should give priority to our practices of piety. God deserves the first place in our list of things to do.
- We should punctually follow our schedules at home and in the workplace.
- Let us get up at a set time, living the "heroic minute."
- We should meet carefully our given deadlines and avoid putting work off for the following day.
- Let us inform those who have to know when we cannot be where and when we are expected.

[105] Ibid.

Order

The virtue of order should be lived in material things, in accordance with the motto "A place for everything, and everything in its place." Material order is often a reflection of the inner order in our souls.

23

CHEERFULNESS

Finally, the end product of living the virtues mentioned above is a *cheerfulness* that nothing and nobody can take away from us. The reason for this is that living the Christian life in its fullness, seeking the hidden Lord and finding Him,[106] always comes together with a permanent joy accompanied by a deep peace.

Cheerfulness is part of the will of God for us Christians: "Serve the Lord with gladness." But it is a joy that does not depend on the situation. St. Josemaría says:

It is not the kind we might call physiological good spirits, the happiness of a healthy animal.

You must seek something more: the supernatural happiness that comes from the abandonment of everything and the abandonment of yourself into the loving arms of our Father God.[107]

And also: "You are unhappy? Think: there must be an obstacle between God and me. You will seldom be wrong."[108]

When we truly love the veiled God, exercising faith and hope, we are happy. On occasion, we might even want to sing, for "to

---

[106] See *The Way*, no. 666.
[107] *Friends of God*, no. 12; cf. *The Way*, no. 659.
[108] *The Way*, no. 662.

THE LITTLE MANUAL FOR SPIRITUAL GROWTH

sing is proper to lovers." A life of faith, hope, and love is a great life, and it is an indicator of a deep interior contact with God. It is impossible to be truly joyful if we do not converse with God.

As St. Josemaría says:

> Cheerfulness is a necessary consequence of our divine filiation, of knowing that our Father God loves us with a love of predilection, that He holds us up and helps us and forgives us.
>
> Remember this and never forget it: even if it should seem at times that everything around you is collapsing, in fact nothing is collapsing at all, because God does not lose battles.[109]

Thus, even when confronted with huge problems, we are to realize that, as St. Paul said, "In everything God works for good with those who love him" (Rom. 8:28).

Thus, his insistent advice makes sense: "Rejoice in the Lord always; again I will say, Rejoice" (Phil. 4:4). We should always look on the bright side of things. What seems most overwhelming in life is not really so dark, so unbearable. If you get down to specifics, you will not draw pessimistic conclusions. We are to get out from a negative overall view, and we must trust the Lord.

Furthermore, it is important to reject sadness, for it can easily convince us that we need some consolation, a break, a compensation that could open the door to sinful actions. A sad soul is predisposed to sin. It is important to be sincere about this matter in our examination of conscience and in our spiritual direction.

Sadness is often caused by an excessive love of self. Conversely, self-forgetfulness for the sake of God and others generates joy in us. It is a type of joy that the Lord wants us to have, and it can be

---

[109] *The Forge*, no. 332.

earned by piety, sincerity, and self-mastery. The reason for the latter is that the sweetest victory is the victory over oneself.

As in everything else, in order to acquire the virtue of cheerfulness, we are to ask the help of our Lady. She is invoked as the *cause of our joy!*

EPILOGUE

Dear reader, we will part ways here. I have made some suggestions that were also recommendations made by St. Josemaría Escrivá, and which he himself lived with heroic alacrity. They were made taking into account the free will that the veiled God has granted to all of us. In other words, these are only invitations to do all these things freely *because we want to*; because we are truly convinced that it is fitting for us to do them. It is precisely this great gift of liberty that opens the door to merit, keeps our human dignity, and supports our hope for the great prize of the vision of the concealed Examiner when the test of this life will be over and the covering curtain will, at last, be forever removed.

These suggestions are not meant to be followed in their totality on the very first day. Almost always, a certain period of time will be needed to incorporate them gradually into our daily habits. St. Josemaría, speaking on the advancement of spiritual life, refers to this as "an inclined plane." In the attempt to make step-by-step progress, the help of a spiritual director cannot be overemphasized. It is certainly very helpful to have someone who, with prudence and in a demanding fashion, will encourage us to move forward towards the supreme goal of *falling in love with the hidden God*.

SUGGESTED PRAYERS

St. Josemaría's Morning Offering

All my thoughts, all my words, all the actions of this day, I offer to You, Lord, and all out of Love.

St. Josemaría's Blessing for a Trip

Through the intercession of the Blessed Mary, may I have a good trip. May the Lord be in my journey; and may His angel accompany me!

St. Josemaría's Spiritual Communion

I wish, Lord, to receive You with the purity, humility, and devotion with which your most holy Mother received you, with the spirit and fervor of the saints.

Angelus

The Angel of the Lord declared to Mary:
And she conceived of the Holy Spirit.

Hail Mary, full of grace, the Lord is with thee; blessed art thou among women and blessed is the fruit of thy womb, Jesus. Holy Mary, Mother of God, pray for us sinners, now and at the hour of our death. Amen.

Behold the handmaid of the Lord:
Be it done unto me according to Thy word.

Hail Mary . . .

And the Word was made Flesh:
And dwelt among us.

Hail Mary . . .

Pray for us, O Holy Mother of God, that we may be made
worthy of the promises of Christ.

Let us pray. Pour forth, we beseech Thee, O Lord, Thy grace
into our hearts; that we, to whom the Incarnation of Christ,
Thy Son, was made known by the message of an angel,
may by His Passion and Cross be brought to the glory of His
Resurrection, through the same Christ Our Lord. Amen.

Regina Coeli

Queen of Heaven, rejoice, alleluia.
For He whom you did merit to bear, alleluia.
Has risen, as he said, alleluia.
Pray for us to God, alleluia.
Rejoice and be glad, O Virgin Mary, alleluia.
For the Lord has truly risen, alleluia.

Let us pray. O God, who gave joy to the world through the
Resurrection of Thy Son, our Lord Jesus Christ, grant, we
beseech Thee, that through the intercession of the Virgin
Mary, His Mother, we may obtain the joys of everlasting life.
Through the same Christ our Lord. Amen.

Suggested Prayers

St. Michael Prayer

St. Michael the Archangel, defend us in battle. Be our defense against the wickedness and snares of the devil. May God rebuke him, we humbly pray; and do you, O Prince of the heavenly hosts, by the power of God, thrust into hell Satan, and all the evil spirits, who prowl about the world seeking the ruin of souls. Amen.

Guardian Angel Prayer

Angel of God, my guardian dear, to whom His love commits me here, ever this day [or: night] be at my side, to light and guard, to rule and guide. Amen.

Memorare

Remember, O most gracious Virgin Mary, that never was it known that anyone who fled to your protection, implored your help, or sought your intercession was left unaided. Inspired by this confidence, I fly unto you, O Virgin of virgins, my Mother. To you I come, before you I stand, sinful and sorrowful. O Mother of the Word Incarnate, despise not my petitions, but, in your mercy, hear and answer me. Amen.

Hail Holy Queen

Hail, Holy Queen, Mother of mercy, our life, our sweetness, and our hope. To you do we cry, poor banished children of Eve. To you do we send up our sighs, mourning, and weeping in this valley of tears. Turn, then, most gracious advocate, your eyes of mercy toward us, and after this, our exile, show unto us the blessed fruit of your womb, Jesus. O clement, O loving, O sweet Virgin Mary.

Te Deum

O God, we praise Thee, and acknowledge Thee to
  be the supreme Lord.
Everlasting Father, all the earth worships Thee.
All the Angels, the heavens and all angelic powers,
All the Cherubim and Seraphim, continuously cry to Thee:
Holy, Holy, Holy, Lord God of Hosts!
Heaven and earth are full of the Majesty of Thy glory.
The glorious choir of the Apostles,
The wonderful company of Prophets,
The white-robed army of Martyrs, praise Thee.
Holy Church throughout the world acknowledges Thee:
The Father of infinite Majesty;
Thy adorable, true and only Son;
Also the Holy Spirit, the Comforter.
O Christ, Thou art the King of glory!
Thou art the everlasting Son of the Father.
When Thou tookest it upon Thyself to deliver man,
Thou didst not disdain the Virgin's womb.
Having overcome the sting of death, Thou opened the
Kingdom of Heaven to all believers.
Thou sittest at the right hand of God in the glory of the Father.
We believe that Thou willst come to be our Judge.
We, therefore, beg Thee to help Thy servants whom Thou
hast redeemed with Thy Precious Blood.
Let them be numbered with Thy Saints in everlasting glory.

V. Save Thy people, O Lord, and bless Thy inheritance!
R. Govern them, and raise them up forever.

V. Every day we thank Thee.
R. And we praise Thy Name forever, yes, forever and ever.

Suggested Prayers

V. O Lord, deign to keep us from sin this day.
R. Have mercy on us, O Lord, have mercy on us.

V. Let Thy mercy, O Lord, be upon us, for we have hoped in Thee.
R. O Lord, in Thee I have put my trust; let me never be put to shame.

Angelic Trisagion

In the name of the Father, and of the Son, and of the Holy Spirit. Amen.

V. Lord, open my lips.
R. And my mouth shall declare Thy praise.

V. O God, come to my assistance.
R. O Lord, make haste to help me.

V. Glory be to the Father, and to the Son, and to the Holy Spirit,
R. As it was in the beginning, is now and will be forever. Amen.

(The decade below is recited three times, once for each member of the Trinity.)

All: Holy God! Holy Strong One! Holy Immortal One, have mercy upon us.

V. Our Father, who art in heaven, hallowed be Thy name. Thy kingdom come. Thy will be done, on earth as it is in Heaven. Give us this day our daily bread and forgive us our trespasses as we forgive those who trespass against us. And lead us not into temptation, but deliver us from evil. Amen.

(The following part of the decade is repeated nine times.)

V. To Thee, O Blessed Trinity, be praise, and honor, and thanksgiving, for ever and ever!
R. Holy, holy, holy Lord, God of hosts. Heaven and earth are filled with Thy glory.

V. Glory be to the Father, and to the Son, and to the Holy Spirit,
R. As it was in the beginning, is now and will be forever. Amen.

Antiphon

God the Father unbegotten, only-begotten Son, and Holy Spirit, the Comforter; holy and undivided Trinity, with all our hearts we acknowledge Thee: Glory to Thee forever.
V. Let us bless the Father, and the Son with the Holy Spirit.
R. Be praised and exalted above all things forever.

Let us pray: Almighty, ever-living God, who has permitted us Thy servants, in our profession of the true faith, to acknowledge the glory of the eternal Trinity, and in the power of that majesty to adore the Unity, grant, that by steadfastness in this same faith, we may be ever guarded against all adversity: through Christ our Lord.

All: Amen.

All: Set us free, save us, vivify us, O Blessed Trinity!

Athanasian Creed

Whosoever will be saved, before all things it is necessary that he hold the Catholic Faith. Which Faith except everyone do keep whole and undefiled, without doubt he shall perish everlastingly. And the Catholic Faith is this: that we worship one God in Trinity and Trinity in Unity. Neither confounding the Persons, nor dividing the Substance. For there is one Person of the Father, another of the Son, and another of the Holy Ghost. But the Godhead of the Father, of the Son and of the Holy Ghost is all One, the Glory Equal, the Majesty Co-Eternal. Such as the Father is, such is the Son, and such is the Holy Ghost. The Father Uncreate, the Son Uncreate, and the Holy Ghost Uncreate. The Father Incomprehensible, the Son Incomprehensible, and the Holy Ghost Incomprehensible. The Father Eternal, the Son Eternal, and the Holy Ghost Eternal, and yet they are not Three Eternals but One Eternal. As also there are not Three Uncreated, nor Three Incomprehensibles, but One Uncreated, and One Incomprehensible. So likewise the Father is Almighty, the Son Almighty, and the Holy Ghost Almighty. And yet they are not Three Almighties but One Almighty.

Prayer Taught by the Angel at Fatima

My God, I believe, I adore, I hope, and I love You. I ask pardon for all those who do not believe, do not adore, do not hope, and do not love You.

BIBLIOGRAPHY

Abad, Javier, and Eugenio Fenoy. *Children: Their Training, Formation and Education*. Manila: Sinag-tala Publishers, 1995.

Bonelli, Raphael. *Palabra*. Madrid: Ediciones Palabra, July 2012.

Boylan, Eugene. *The Spiritual Life of the Priest*. Westminster, MD: Newman Press, 1961.

de Prada, Andres Vazquez. *The Founder of Opus Dei*. Vol. 2. New York: Scepter Publishers, 2003.

Knox, Ronald. *A Retreat for Lay People*. Lagos: Criterion Publishers, 2005.

Navarro, J. Lopez. *The Joys and Travails of a Large Family*. Manila: Sinag-tala Publishers, 1975.

Ramírez, Antonio María. *Comprometerse*. Madrid: Ediciones Palabra, 2007.

Rhonheimer, Martin. *You Are the Light of the World*. Manila: Sinag-tala Publishers, 2010.

Stenson, James B. *Reading: Learning to Choose*. London: Scepter Publishers, 1984.

Trese, Leo. *The Faith Explained*. Manila: Sinag-tala Publishers, 2008.

Works of Saints, Popes, and Church Documents

Augustine. *Confessions*. New York: Image Books, 1960.

———. *De Civitate Dei*.

Benedict XVI. *Jesus of Nazareth.* New York: Doubleday, 2007.

Compendium of the Catechism of the Catholic Church. Manila: Episcopal Commission on Catechesis and Catholic Education, 2007.

Escrivá, Josemaría. *Christ Is Passing By.* Manila: Sinag-tala Publishers, 2000.

——. *Conversations with Monsignor Escrivá de Balaguer.* Manila: Sinag-tala Publishers, 1985.

——. *The Forge.* Manila: Sinag-tala Publishers, 2000.

——. *Friends of God.* Manila: Sinag-tala Publishers, 2000.

——. *Furrow.* Manila: Sinag-tala Publishers, 2000.

——. *Holy Rosary.* Manila: Sinag-tala Publishers, 2000.

——. *The Way.* Manila: Sinag-tala Publishers, 1985.

——. *The Way of the Cross.* London: Scepter Press, 1982.

John XXIII. Encyclical on the Rosary *Grata Recordatio.* September 26, 1959.

John Paul II. *Prayer for Priests on Holy Thursday.* March 25, 1982.

Leonard of Port Maurice. *The Hidden Treasure of the Holy Mass.* Rockford, IL: TAN Books,1952.

Paul VI. *Discourse.* October 10, 1964.

Pius XII. Encyclical *Ad Apostolorum Principis.* June 29, 1958.

Sacred Congregation of the Sacraments. *Immensae Caritatis.* January 29, 1973.

Second Vatican Council. Pastoral Constitution on the Church in the Modern World *Gaudium et Spes.* December 7, 1965.

Teresa of Jesus. *The Life of Teresa of Jesus: The Autobiography of St. Teresa of Ávila.* Translated and edited by E. Allison Peers. New York: Doubleday, 1960.

ABOUT THE AUTHOR

Born in Vic (Barcelona), Spain, in 1932, John C. Portavella obtained a master's degree in chemistry at the University of Barcelona. In 1958, he earned a doctorate in canon law from the University of Santo Tomas (Angelicum) in Rome and was ordained priest in 1959 for the Opus Dei prelature. He was asked by the founder, St. Josemaría Escrivá, to exercise ministry in the United States and to help in the apostolic work there. He remained in the United States until 1967, when the founder asked him to serve in the Philippines.

He is currently doing pastoral work at the University of Asia and the Pacific, in Pasig City, Metro Manila.

Sophia Institute

Sophia Institute is a nonprofit institution that seeks to nurture the spiritual, moral, and cultural life of souls and to spread the Gospel of Christ in conformity with the authentic teachings of the Roman Catholic Church.

Sophia Institute Press fulfills this mission by offering translations, reprints, and new publications that afford readers a rich source of the enduring wisdom of mankind.

Sophia Institute also operates two popular online Catholic resources: CrisisMagazine.com and CatholicExchange.com.

Crisis Magazine provides insightful cultural analysis that arms readers with the arguments necessary for navigating the ideological and theological minefields of the day. *Catholic Exchange* provides world news from a Catholic perspective as well as daily devotionals and articles that will help readers to grow in holiness and live a life consistent with the teachings of the Church.

In 2013, Sophia Institute launched Sophia Institute for Teachers to renew and rebuild Catholic culture through service to Catholic education. With the goal of nurturing the spiritual, moral, and cultural life of souls, and an abiding respect for the role and work of teachers, we strive to provide materials and programs that are at once enlightening to the mind and ennobling to the heart; faithful and complete, as well as useful and practical.

Sophia Institute gratefully recognizes the Solidarity Association for preserving and encouraging the growth of our apostolate over the course of many years. Without their generous and timely support, this book would not be in your hands.

www.SophiaInstitute.com
www.CatholicExchange.com
www.CrisisMagazine.com
www.SophiaInstituteforTeachers.org

Sophia Institute Press® is a registered trademark of Sophia Institute. Sophia Institute is a tax-exempt institution as defined by the Internal Revenue Code, Section 501(c)(3). Tax I.D. 22-2548708.